Favourite Bears
to make & treasure

12 original, easy-to-make designs

Favourite Bears
to make & treasure

12 original, easy-to-make designs

Julia Jones

DRAGON'S WORLD

Dragon's World Ltd
Limpsfield
Surrey RH8 ODY
Great Britain

First published by Dragon's World Ltd, 1995

© Dragon's World Ltd, 1995
© Text Julia Jones, 1995

Editor: Cathy Meeus
Art Director: John Strange
Designer: Megra Mitchell
Photographer: David Parmiter
Editorial Director: Pippa Rubinstein

No part of this book may be reproduced in any form or by any means, electronic or mechanical, including information storage and retrieval systems, without permission in writing from Dragon's World Ltd, except by a reviewer who may quote brief passages in a review.

All rights reserved.

The catalogue record for this book is available from the British Library.

ISBN 1 85028 208 0

With the exception of Samuel, featured on page 100, the instructions in this book are for collector's bears, not toys. Although the fabrics used conform to British Standard Safety Regulations governing the production of toys, the joints and eyes are not suitable for children under the age of 10 years.

The patterns in this book are intended only for personal use by readers. Any commercial use of these designs is an infringement of copyright. Readers seeking copyright permission should contact the author and publishers directly.

CONTENTS

Introduction 6
Materials and Equipment 8
Fabrics and Fillings 9
Other Materials 13
Essential Equipment 16
Your First Bear 20
Making the Basic Bear 20
Tiny 34
Charles 40
Claude 46
Astbury 52
Little Roger 58
Bertie 64
Rose 72
Theodore 78
Edward 86
Oscar 94
Samuel 100
Bear Care 106
Useful Addresses 108
Further Reading 110
Index 111
Acknowledgements 112

INTRODUCTION

The teddy bear as we know him today has, perhaps surprisingly, existed only since the beginning of the 20th century. Nowadays, his familiar, comforting image can be seen everywhere, innocently endorsing items as diverse as breakfast cereals and postal services.

The first teddy bear was born in 1903, the inspiration of a Russian immigrant to New York, named Morris Michtom. However, the history of bear-making really begins some 50 years earlier, across the Atlantic in the small German town of Giengen an der Brenze, near Stuttgart, when a baby girl called Margarete Steiff was born. Disabled by polio from an early age, she was nevertheless determined to earn her own living. Using a specially adapted sewing machine, she started to make elephant pin cushions. The business quickly grew, and diversified into soft toys until she was able to offer employment to her five nephews. The company became a leading name in toymaking, exporting toys around the world. In 1898 Steiff produced its first bear, a skittle bear that stood on a wooden base.

Around this time, Margarete's youngest nephew, Richard, was studying at a local college, spending his spare hours at the circus and zoo, where he sketched animals to add to the constantly growing range. A jointed bear was sent to the Leipzig Toy Fair of 1903. Orders flowed in and success was guaranteed.

TEDDY'S BEAR

In November 1902, the American political cartoonist Clifford Berryman published a cartoon featuring President Theodore Roosevelt on an unsuccessful bear hunt in Mississippi. Although details vary from account to account, the story behind the scene was that the President, having failed to 'bag' a single animal, was offered a tethered cub by eager colleagues. The offer was declined with the allegedly touching comment

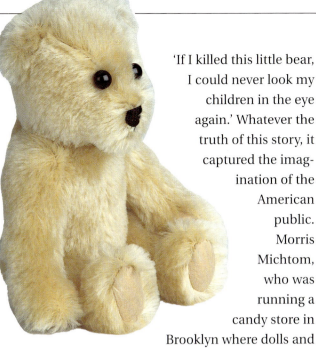

'If I killed this little bear, I could never look my children in the eye again.' Whatever the truth of this story, it captured the imagination of the American public. Morris Michtom, who was running a candy store in Brooklyn where dolls and soft toys were displayed in the shop window from time to time to attract customers, was one of the first to recognize the worth of a good story.

He wrote to the President asking permission to name a toy bear 'Teddy's Bear', with the advertising slogan 'A Toy for Boys.' The President agreed and the 'teddy' was born.

Today, bears are being made all over the world in greater numbers than ever before. Craft-workers and artists are devoting their time and talents to the never-ending search for the perfect bear, and most well-established companies are delving into their archives to produce limited-edition replicas of their most attractive characters.

Prices for antique bears at auction are soaring, putting the most sought-after examples out of the range of most collectors. However, as enthusiasm grows, more and more 'arctophiles' (literally – friends of bears) are turning to specialist suppliers and designers for the knowledge and materials that will enable them to make their own.

BEAR APPEAL

What is it about the teddy bear that engenders this universal appeal? Psychologists tell us that with his large, round head and bright, innocent eyes, he closely imitates the characteristics of any baby animal, thereby arousing our basic protective instincts. With arms outstretched to greet us, he offers unconditional affection.

Who but a bear can be totally trusted not to judge, criticize or condemn? For children the teddy bear is endowed with a magic that can soothe bumps and bruises as well as hurt feelings. Many bears have accompanied their owners into adulthood, helping them to face those difficult and dangerous times.

The bears in this book are designed to be made with love to give as a gift – to be cherished in the years to come. Comprehensive instructions are given for each bear-making project, but as your confidence develops, do not be afraid to experiment. Pads, paws and ears can be personalized with scraps of fabric saved, for example, from a favourite garment or a wedding dress. The scope for adding individual features is as boundless as your imagination.

As you work, you will, no doubt, soon realize that no two bears look quite the same, even though they may be made from an identical pattern and fabric. Somewhere along the line, each bear takes a hand, expressing his own individuality through his maker's skill. This is the delightful adventure you will surely discover as you begin to make your own favourite bears.

Materials & Equipment

One of the most important decisions you will make when embarking on making a bear is choosing the fabric. You first need to understand a little of the vast range of bear-making fabrics available, as this choice will affect the look of your finished bear. For a high-quality bear it is important to use only the best possible, natural materials. These, although more expensive than sythentics, will give you an end result of which you can be proud. A particular type of fabric is recommended for each of the bears in this book, but you can vary the effect by using alternative fabrics if you wish. Within reason any bear can be made from any fabric. The only exception is that for very small bears a non-pile, short pile or 'miniature' bear fabric should be used.

In general, short-pile fabrics produce a more traditional looking bear, while textured mohairs give a more up-to-date look. For a feminine-looking bear you could try a 'feathered' or 'string' weave fabric in pale or pastel colours.

When you are making your selection, remember that the quality and appearance of the 'fur' will play a decisive role in the final appearance of your bear and will ultimately affect how long he or she will survive. Pay special attention to the quality of the weave. A loosely woven material may be difficult to sew, particularly when ladder stitching. A closely woven fabric, although more difficult to cut and tack, produces a better finish.

Fabrics and Fillings

Buying Fabric

As prices vary considerably from stockist to stockist, check with a number of suppliers before making a decision. Don't forget to take into account possible charges for postage, packing and, perhaps, insurance. Fur fabric is generally 54 inches (135 cm) wide, unless otherwise stated. Careful placing and cutting of your templates will help you get the most from your fabric. Don't throw away any trimmings, however small – they may be useful later for cutting ears, or tiny arms and legs.

When ordering by post, it makes sense to buy as much as you think you will need for several bears at one time, thus cutting down the postage and packing charges that would be incurred on several smaller parcels. In addition, large quantities can often be purchased at a discount.

Safety First

If you are making bears as toys in the United Kingdom do check that your chosen fabric conforms to British Standard Regulations BS5665 Parts 1, 2 and 3. In all other countries, check with your own Safety Standards Department and with a reputable supplier. All materials used for children's toys must conform to these regulations, including stuffing, joints, eyes and, where applicable, noses.

Fabrics for Bear Bodies

The fleece of many different animals can be used to weave fur pile fabrics. These natural materials are infinitely preferable to synthetics for making collectors' bears. Fur fabrics can be purchased with a pile length from about $1/8$ inch to one inch (4–25 mm) and in a variety of finishes, including swirl, V-wave, distressed and antiqued.

The qualities of the most popular bear-making fabrics are described here.

Alpaca is the wool of the Peruvian llama. The fleece is fine and soft, and produces a warm, luxurious fabric. It is, however, expensive. Fur fabric made from alpaca can make an extremely attractive bear. It is often combined with other natural fibres to produce a more hard-wearing material.

Cashmere is the fleece of a type of goat found in the Indian province of Kashmir in the Western Himalayas and in Tibet. The fleece is spun and woven in the same manner as mohair, but produces a softer, more supple and, therefore, more delicate fabric. Because true cashmere is very expensive, fine sheep's wool yarn is often used in imitation. A bear made from real cashmere feels soft, warm and infinitely huggable. Cashmere yarn can also be combined with silk and wool.

A selection of fur fabrics. From left to right: 100 per cent German mohair (dense, straight pile); synthethic mock mohair; 'windswept-look' German mohair; synthetic, soft-pile knitted-back.

MATERIALS & EQUIPMENT

Mohair (Angora) is the fleece of a breed of goat that was originally found only in the Angora region of Turkey. The term mohair is derived from the Arabic word meaning 'select' or 'choice' – a reference to the fabric's hard-wearing, soft and luxurious properties. Mohair has always been the first choice for quality bear making. The majority of mohair production today comes from the Americas and South Africa, where the animals are farmed commercially. An imitation mohair fabric is available woven from an inexpensive wool and cotton mix. This can be useful for practice purposes for those new to bear making.

Silk Spun from the cocoon of the silk worm grub, silk is undoubtedly one of the most beautiful materials. Unfortunately, it is not as durable as mohair and therefore needs careful handling. Do not expose fabrics containing silk to full sunlight or to sources of heat such as radiators or they will deteriorate. A bear made from this material should be kept in an atmosphere that is not over dry otherwise the delicate fibres will weaken and become brittle, and may eventually disintegrate. Some silk woven-pile fabrics also have an unstable and loosely woven ground fabric. This may have a tendency to shed fibres. Do not use a silk-based fabric unless the bear is to be kept in suitable conditions and subjected to very little handling. If you do decide to use such a fabric, lightly brush or comb the pile to test its stability. Although all cut fur fabrics will shed a little pile, beware of any whose loss seems excessive.

Synthetic fabrics are the best choice for beginners who may feel unsure of their abilities and do not want to make mistakes with expensive materials. They are also essential for making washable and fire-retardant children's toys. The quality of synthetic fabrics at the upper end of the price range is very high and many specialist suppliers carry a range of such materials that provide excellent alternatives to the more expensive natural fibres. Many synthetic furs have a glossy appearance, similar to that of real fur and will produce beautiful bears at a fraction of the cost of real mohair. Synthetic fabrics and fillings are recommended for bears that are to be given to sufferers from asthma or other allergies. Synthetic fabrics have a knitted ground that may distort if stuffed with woodwool. Synthetic fillings are therefore the best choice.

Beware of cheap synthetic fabrics available from non-specialist outlets. Even when working

This page, from left to right: (top) cotton and viscose, knitted-back fabric; straight-pile German mohair; V-weave German mohair; knitted-pile synthetic fabric; coney knitted-pile synthetic fabric; (bottom) knitted-pile acrylic fabric; German woven mohair; crushed-pile German woven mohair.
Facing page, materials for paws and pads, from left to right: leather; three colours of suedette; four colours of German woollen felt.

to a tight budget, buy your synthetic fabric from a specialist, who knows how the fabric will handle and can give you good advice.

Lining Fabric

When working with a fabric that has a loosely woven ground or with fragile fabrics such as silk or cashmere, which may be damaged by prolonged contact with an abrasive stuffing medium, it is advisable to line each section of the bear with a firm, smooth material such as calico. Light-weight curtain lining fabric is a good substitute if calico is not available. See the instructions for making *Charles* on page 40.

Materials for Pads and Paws

Suede, leather, velvet and felt are the most common materials for pads and paws. However, other fabrics can also be used. Silk or cashmere are suitable for luxury bears that are likely to receive little handling.

Suede and suedette can often be purchased in colours that complement a particular stockist's range of mohair fabrics. For most bear-makers, it is most economical to buy it by the 12-inch (30-cm) square. However, if you intend to make a large number of bears, full hides are available at a discount. Alternatively, smaller leather pieces can be obtained from leather specialists. Glove-makers often sell 'off cut' bargain bags. This is probably the cheapest means of obtaining high quality, soft leather, but supply and colours are somewhat erratic and continuity cannot be relied upon.

Felt can be made either from wool or from acrylic fibres. Where possible, always choose the natural woollen fabric, as the colours are generally softer and more traditional. Felt used for soft toys should carry the necessary safety standard approval.

Controlling Fraying

Before drawing out the pattern pieces, it is advisable to apply a backing of iron-on interfacing to fabrics that are likely to fray or that may be difficult to handle. This gives a firmer finish to pads and paws and can be used for added body throughout the bear. A commercially produced 'fray check' is also a useful addition to your work box. Applied to the fabric, this seals cut edges and prevents unravelling.

MATERIALS & EQUIPMENT

German felt is recognized to be the finest quality available and can be purchased in colours similar to those used by Steiff and other famous factories. It is no coincidence that the Steiff factory was established and still flourishes in a town renowned for its felt manufacture. As felt is made by a process that locks and tangles its fibres together, rather than by weaving, it has no nap or pile. It can, therefore, be cut on either side and in any direction, keeping waste to a minimum.

Upholstery velvet and velveteen create a luxury look for pads and paws and can also be used to produce a complete bear. Crushed or panné velvet is particularly attractive. To make such fabric easier to handle, it may be necessary to back it with a woven iron-on interfacing before drawing around the templates. This reduces the risk of stretching and improves the finished appearance of the bear.

PROTECTING AGAINST MOTHS

All natural fibres are subject to attack by moths and other insects. Any bear kept on permanent display will benefit from an occasional spray with a fabric-safe insect repellant. If in any doubt, ask the advice of your fabric supplier or the textiles curator at your nearest museum. This is especially important if you are the proud owner of an ancient bear.

FILLING MATERIALS

Fillings for use in children's toys must conform to safety regulations (see page 9). However, a wide range of suitable products are available that meet these standards.

Synthetic fibres Polyester and acrylic fillings can be purchased in small quantities from most craft shops. Larger quantities can be obtained more cheaply by mail order or from a specialist supplier. Always buy a small amount initially to find out if the product suits your needs. If you like it, you can then buy in bulk.

Different synthetic fibres produce fillings with widely differing properties. A Dacron filling, for instance, gives a more springy feel than some polyesters. However, the best man-made filling for bears is probably the light, springy acrylic sold by most bear-materials suppliers. This may be slightly more expensive, but gives excellent results.

Plastic pellets *Theodore*, *Edward* and *Bertie* have arms and legs filled with tiny, round, plastic pellets, giving a 'floppy' feel. These can be combined with woodwool or synthetic fibres and are light and easy to use. Stuff paws and pads with a light polyester or wool filling, and pack polyester filling tightly around the joint heads before adding the pellets. Pellets should not be used in bears intended as children's toys.

Kapok is made from the cotton-like fibres that surround the seeds of a tropical tree. Small bears can be entirely stuffed with this natural material, or it can be combined with woodwool, pellets, or synthetic fibres. As the fine strands of kapok can easily become airborne during the stuffing process, asthma sufferers should wear a mask when using this or any other material that may irritate the lungs.

Fleece Sheep's wool (fleece) that has been carefully washed and cleaned, can be bought in bulk by mail order from specialist spinning or toy-making suppliers. However, when buying a fleece directly from the farmer, or when gathering wool from hedgerows, always ensure that you wash it thoroughly before use. Remove any twigs or soiled areas before washing in warm water and a liquid detergent. Rinse well with plenty of running water. Place in an old pillow case, which can be pegged out on the washing line or dried in a tumble drier. When dry gently tease out the fibres until they are fluffy.

Small balls of fleece packed into the nose tip and paws allow the needle to pass more easily through the fabric when embroidering the nose, mouth and claws.

Woodwool Fine woodwool shavings can be purchased from specialist suppliers. It is sold by weight and is compressed into loose blocks. Keep it in a large, sturdy box. Shake out the blocks and remove any large or sharp splinters of wood before use. Woodwool can be combined with other fillings, including sawdust for a traditional collectors' bear.

Sawdust is a filling that has fallen from favour with modern bear-makers. It can, however, be combined with woodwool for a firm filling or used on its own. Sawdust can be obtained cheaply from timber yards and should be inserted into your bear through a plastic funnel in the same way as plastic pellets. Sawdust is not suitable for toy bears or for bears for asthma sufferers.

Filling materials, from left to right: woodwool; polyester filling; plastic pellets.

OTHER MATERIALS

THREAD

Always buy the best quality thread available. Nothing is more depressing than finding seams on an otherwise delightful bear splitting because of poor quality thread. Thread is made in almost as many colours as fabrics and it should prove a fairly simple matter to find a thread that matches your fabric. If a perfect match is unobtainable, choose a shade slightly darker than the fabric. In normal household sewing, a contrasting thread colour is recommended for tacking. However, when making a bear, always use tacking thread that is a similar colour to the fabric, as this will be less noticeable should any strands be inadvertently left in the seams.

Mercerized cotton is the most useful thread for general sewing. It is strong and smooth and is ideal for most hand and machine sewing jobs.

Nylon thread is very strong and can be used with synthetic fabrics and is also useful for ladder-stitching and for attaching ears and eyes. When machine sewing with this thread, it may be necessary to use a looser upper and lower tension than normal to prevent puckering. The instruction book for your sewing machine should also give the manufacturer's recommendations regarding threads and needles.

Buttonhole twist and other heavy-duty threads are recommended for machine-stitching the seams of some of the larger bears, for ladder-stitching and for attaching ears and eyes. These threads can be pulled tightly without snapping and will withstand a great deal of pressure. Some linen carpet and leatherwork threads are extra strong and very useful, although the colour range is somewhat limited.

MATERIALS & EQUIPMENT

Embroidery threads in cotton, wool and silk are recommended for embroidering features. A wide variety of colours and textures are available and personal preference can govern your choice. When using six-strand embroidery threads, individual instructions indicate the number of strands required.

Viscose thread is more durable than silk and gives a similar high gloss appearance. However, most bear-makers prefer the traditional appeal of natural materials.

JOINTS FOR ARMS AND LEGS

Most quality bears are jointed using hardboard or 'crown' joints. These consist of two hardboard or leather discs, two metal washers and a 'split' or 'cotter' pin. Some hardboard joints are fitted with bolts that have locking nuts and washers. Hardboard joints are available in metric sizes from 15 mm to 88 mm. However, tiny 10 mm rigid cardboard joints are available for miniature bears. These joints are not suitable for use in bears intended as children's toys.

> ### SAFETY-LOCKING JOINTS
> In the 1950s, several toy firms were experimenting with safety locking joints. Today all children's toys must use joints which conform to strict safety regulations. Most bear-making suppliers stock such joints. These are made of plastic and consist of a flat, mushroom shaped joint, the shank of which is pushed through the fabric. A few strands of the fabric may need to be cut to make a small hole. Once in position, a plastic disc is placed onto the shank, followed by a metal or plastic washer, which is forced down to form a permanent joint. As this can require a great deal of pressure, a cotton reel or safety tool can be used for extra purchase. You need to be very careful when positioning a safety joint, because once assembled, they are impossible to undo.
>
> Safety-locking joints are available in metric sizes from 20 mm to 65 mm. Some are held by metal washers, while others have ridged stems which hold the plastic washer in position, preventing the discs from loosening during use.

Selection of hardboard joints and plastic safety-locking joints.

Eyes

Boot buttons Manufacturers of early bears used black wooden or papier mâché boot buttons. Today reproduction boot buttons are available in a wide range of sizes. It is, however, still possible to buy cards of antique boot buttons, which are perfect for very special bears.

Glass eyes are available in many colours. For bears the most suitable colours are plain black or amber and brown with black pupils. Glass eyes are supplied either in pairs attached by a thin straight wire, which must be cut and bent before use, or singly with a wire loop or 'bail' back fitting. Suppliers often offer a discount for large orders.

Beads and buttons have been used in the past for bears eyes. Occasionally, these would be backed with circles of red or orange felt, making the bear look rather ferocious.

Plastic safety eyes must be used for any bear intended as a children's toy. These can be obtained from most craft shops and mail order craft suppliers. They come in a wide range of colours and sizes. Safety eyes must be fitted before the head is stuffed and great care should be taken to get the position right first time. It may be necessary to cut a few strands of the ground fabric to enable the thick shank to pass through. The eye is held by a plastic or metal washer which should be forced into position as tightly as possible. It is possible to purchase an eye tool for this purpose. Some suppliers, particularly those in the United States, offer plastic eyes that have been designed to cause a depression in the fabric when correctly assembled. This gives the appearance of a natural eye socket.

Noses

Bear-makers often try to personalize and distinguish their bears by the distinctive and original methods chosen to form the nose and mouth. A large proportion of a bear's appeal depends on the quality of its features. Most traditional bears have noses and mouths which have been embroidered using cotton or silk thread. Noses can also be cut from circles of fabric, felt or leather. A variety of plastic moulded safety noses are available, which can be used for children's toys, but these would not be appropriate for collectors' bears.

Bear Voices

Over the years many devices have been used to give bears a 'voice'. These include flat and cylindrical squeakers, hardboard and plastic growlers in various sizes, bells, musical movements, and tinklers.

Musical boxes The most complex and expensive bear voices are musical boxes, which play tunes as diverse as 'The Wedding March' and 'Jingle Bells'. It is usually possible to fit a bear made to commemorate a special occasion with a device that plays an appropriate tune. While most boxes are operated by winding the mechanism with a key, some modern versions are fitted with an inexpensive push button starter. The price of a musical box is usually governed by the number of notes it will play. Instructions for fitting a musical box are given for *Edward* on page 86.

Growlers consist of a small cardboard cylinder, containing a weighted bellows. As the growler is tilted, air is expressed through the small holes in the end of the tube, causing a deep 'growl' to be emitted. The similarity of this sound to a real life bear is debatable, but a growler is, nevertheless, the traditional choice for 'speaking' bears. The body of a bear should be well-stuffed with woodwool before the growler is inserted.

SPECTACLES

Some mail order suppliers are now offering bear-sized spectacles and sunglasses in a variety of styles and shades. Indeed, the choice is so wide that your bear can now proudly sport a pair of smart, oval sunglasses with a choice of red- or blue-tinted lenses. Look for good quality items that have a nose pad and hinged side arms.

MATERIALS & EQUIPMENT

Instructions for fitting a growler are given for *Oscar* on page 94.

Squeakers Cheaper and simpler alternatives to the above can be found in a variety of small plastic bellows, which force air through a reed when pressed. These are easy to fit and should be pushed into the stuffing just before the back body opening is closed.

> **SAFETY NOTE**
>
> Hardboard joints, glass eyes, plastic pellets, bells, musical movements and spectacles are not suitable for bears intended as children's toys. Choose safety-approved substitutes for these items or omit them entirely when making children's toys.

ESSENTIAL EQUIPMENT

The equipment needed for bear-making is neither elaborate nor expensive. While all the bears in this book can be sewn entirely by hand, as time is often limited and most of us have access to either a hand or electric sewing machine, most will choose to use a machine for stitching seams. Whatever method you use, stitching must of course be firm and accurate. Miniature bears should, as a general rule, be hand-stitched – the foot of most sewing machines does not readily accommodate the tiny turnings and curves necessary to produce a tiny bear. This is particularly true when stitching tiny footpads and ears.

SEWING MACHINE

A straight-stitch machine is suitable for all bear-making. A reverse facility is useful for fastening threads securely when starting and finishing. This is particularly important for the seams around any stuffing openings, which must be firmly stitched to prevent them pulling apart during stuffing. In order to save time, it is advisable to pre-wind extra bobbins with a selection of coloured threads.

> **CARE OF YOUR MACHINE**
>
> When working with fur fabric it is advisable to oil and clean your machine regularly. The lint produced by the fabric will clog the mechanism unless it is regularly removed. Remove the throat plate of the bobbin case and the bobbin. Insert the vacuum-cleaner nozzle to suck up dust and strands of thread. Clean the feed-dog at the same time, removing any trapped threads.

SCISSORS

The best scissors are made from hot-drop forged steel, which gives a sharp cutting edge which can be regularly re-ground. If you are buying a new pair of scissors, take along a small test piece of fabric. Check the points and the cutting action, using the entire length of the blade. If the blades have not been manufactured correctly the fabric will snag. Look for scissors with blades fastened by a screw that can be easily tightened, rather than rivets which may loosen during use. Buy the best quality you can afford and treat them with care. Set aside a separate pair of all-purpose or craft scissors for cutting paper or card. Scissors will benefit from an occasional oiling around the screw, particularly after cutting fur fabrics which shed fine lint.

Dressmaker's shears have two uneven handles. The small ring is shaped to fit the thumb, the large ring accommodates the second and third fingers. These are designed to enable the lower blade to rest against the cutting surface. Choose shears with 8 to 9 inch (20–22.5 cm) blades. Straight-handled scissors do not cut as accurately as shears.

Electric shears are a boon for bear makers who suffer from arthritis. The ground fabric of some mohair can be fairly stiff and unyielding, causing problems for those with painful joints. However, electric shears have the knack of running out of control, do practice the cutting action on scraps of fabric until you feel sufficiently confident to move on to expensive mohairs.

Straight scissors An alternative to shears for cutting pile fabrics, these should be straight, with two identical handles. Ideally their sharp-pointed blades should be 3 to 6 inches (7.5–15 cm) long.

Embroidery scissors are needed for trimming muzzles and snipping embroidery threads.

Cutting Board

A cutting board is not essential, but can be extremely useful, particularly when cutting backing fabrics with a sharp-bladed knife or scalpel. A self-healing surface remains sound over a long period of use and protects work surfaces from damage. A cutting board can be quickly wiped over from time to time to remove any dust or tailors' chalk.

Stuffing Tools

Stuffing sticks These can be bought from specialist suppliers. For a home-made alternative try a large wooden knitting needle (with the end knob removed), the handle of a wooden spoon or a 6-inch (15-cm) length of dowelling that has been sanded smooth.

Modelling tools For turning and stuffing bears, particularly small ones, a set of boxwood or plastic sculpture modelling tools is extremely useful. These can be purchased from most good art supply shops and can be used in conjunction with a stuffing stick. Boxwood tools are slightly more expensive to buy, but more satisfying to use. They are also more durable.

Tape-measure

Choose an oilcloth or plastic tape-measure that has a metal tip at each end. A spring-loaded measure that recoils into a protective case after use is also an excellent buy, as it does not easily fray or soil. For ease of conversion, choose a measure which shows both Imperial and metric measurements.

Rulers

Transparent 6-inch (15-cm) and 12-inch (30-cm) rulers with $^{1}/_{8}$ in and 1 mm markings are most useful. However, a metal gauge with a sliding marker is also invaluable for checking eye and ear positions, and for measuring the dimensions of embroidered features such as mouths, noses and claws.

Paper and Card

Squared paper If you intend to draw your templates freehand from the charted templates given on the pattern pages in this book, you will need squared paper of the correct size.

Tracing paper You will need medium-weight tracing paper to transfer photocopied pattern pages or template charts to thin card.

Thin card You will need a sheet of thin card or modelling card to make your pattern templates.

Pens and Markers

Keep a variety of pens and markers ready for use on different fabrics and colours. A chalk pencil is undoubtedly the best choice for drawing a fine, accurate line around templates on the reverse side of fur fabric and other bear-making materials. However, because chalk rubs off easily, any permanent pattern instructions such as dart lines and placement positions should be marked in dressmaker's carbon or with a soft-lead pencil.

Tailor's chalk can be purchased in flat square blocks. It is not as easy to use as a pencil, but is available in a range of colours.

Embroidery marker pens can also be useful, but will only transfer onto fairly smooth fabrics. They are not suitable for most fur fabrics, except perhaps those knitted from synthetic fibres.

Dressmaker's carbon can be used with a tracing wheel to mark pattern instructions and notches.

Tracing Wheel

Tracing wheels are available with different wheel attachments. A wooden or plastic handle holds a metal shank to which a rotating wheel is fitted. To use place a sheet of dressmaker's carbon paper face-down over the ground fabric you wish to mark. Position a template over this and, using the wheel, run around the pattern piece, transferring the outline to the fabric beneath.

NEEDLES AND PINS

Always use the sharpest, undamaged needles and pins in your work. These should be of stainless steel. Reject any that are rusty or rough.

Medium-length 'sharps' needles are recommended for general sewing and tacking. Use sizes 6–8 for medium-weight fabrics and sizes 1–5 for heavy materials.

Embroidery or 'crewel' needles are needed for sewing the features. These are similar to 'sharps' but have a large eye through which thicker threads can be passed.

Large, curved upholstery needles are also useful, but not essential, for ladder stitching and for sewing on ears.

Three-cornered, leather and fur needles easily pass through the tough surface of skins, causing little damage, and are therefore useful when working with these materials.

> ### LABELS AND PACKAGING
> Many makers like to identify their bears with their own label. This can provide a professional finishing touch as well as a means of conveying essential safety information.
> White sew-in labels can be ordered to include your name, address, telephone number and the relevant C. E. symbol as required, showing that your goods comply with the EU Toy Safety Directive, 1990. These are essential for toy bears produced commercially. Labels can also be printed in accordance with the International Textile Care Labelling Code, allowing you to choose your own selection of symbols and ensuring that your bear carries his own specific care instructions.

Long, thin 'straw' or millinery needles are sometimes needed for threading tiny beads to make eyes for miniature bears.

Heavy-duty bodkin or stiletto These are invaluable for attaching eyes on large or well stuffed bears.

Sewing-machine needles in several sizes are required. As fur fabric rapidly blunts needle points, remember to replace these regularly or seam quality may be affected.

Pins Pin numbers 15, 16 and 17 are suitable for all but the heaviest fabrics. However, size 14 pins are useful when working with upholstery materials, heavy leathers and densely woven fur pile. A few 'T' pins and long, glass-headed pins are needed for positioning eyes and ears.

THIMBLE

A thimble is essential when working with heavy fabrics and sharp needles. Find one that fits the middle finger of the hand holding the needle snugly. If you find the thimble slips off during working, wet the end of your finger first. The moisture will create suction that will hold the thimble securely in place.

PIN CUSHION

A really decorative addition to your work box is a pretty pin cushion. Choose one with a strong outer covering which has been filled with sawdust or fleece. Always work with a pin cushion, counting your pins out and in to prevent any being lost inside your bear. Sometimes a store-bought pin cushion is provided with its own emery bag, filled with an abrasive substance that will remove rust from needles and pins. If you intend to leave pins in a cushion for any length of time it is always best to keep them in the emery-filled cushion to prevent moisture damage.

PLIERS

A pair of sturdy pliers is essential for making most of the bears in this book. They are used to pull needles through thick layers of fabric, for curling split pins on hardboard joints, and for making loops on the backs of some types of glass eye. Any pointed 'snipe-nosed' pliers are suitable, although the long-pointed, spring-loaded pliers with plastic coated handles are the best. Some pliers also incorporate a wire-cutter, which is useful for breaking split pins on joints that need to be repositioned, and for cutting the wire joining pairs of glass eyes.

Forceps and Tweezers

Medical clamping forceps can be useful (although not essential) for holding small sections when turning miniature bears. These are available by mail order from medical and some bear-making stockists. A pair of tweezers is also invaluable for removing stray strands of cotton.

Brushes

Wire-bristled, wooden-handled teasel brushes are used for brushing up mohair and fluffing out seams. However, these should not be used on certain special-effect piles as such brushing may damage their finish. A strong nylon-bristled nailbrush or toothbrush is recommended for light brushing of delicate pile fabrics and around suede or leather paws, where wire bristles would cause damage. Some suppliers offer deluxe brushes which are specifically designed for use on long-pile fabrics.

Seam Ripper

This tool is a great help for unpicking tacking stitches and badly sewn seams. The use of this tool makes it less likely that you will cut the ground fabric, but even so great care must be taken, particularly when working with delicate fabrics such as loosely woven silks and cashmere.

Stands

Stands are available for bears of various sizes. These enable you to display your bear in an upright position. Heights range from 6 to 20 inches (15–50 cm).

Hand-Sewing and Embroidery Stitches

Straight stitch This single stitch, which can be of any length, is used for hand stitching seams and for the nose, mouth and claws. Unless otherwise stated, an even working tension should be maintained.

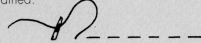

Backstitch This strong stitch has a similar appearance to machine stitching. It can be used for hand stitching seams. Stiches should be small and even.

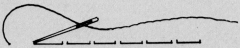

Ladder stitch Used to close seams after stuffing, correctly worked this stitch should be invisible after the working thread has been drawn up. Ladder stitch is worked by taking a tiny straight stitch on either side of the seam alternately. Keep the stuffing well away from the working threads and pull thread up firmly after every few stitches. Experience will soon enable you to judge the most suitable technique for your fabric and thread.

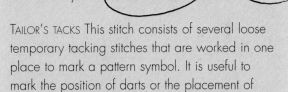

Tailor's tacks This stitch consists of several loose temporary tacking stitches that are worked in one place to mark a pattern symbol. It is useful to mark the position of darts or the placement of joints in this way.

Satin stitch A series of closely placed straight stitches. Stitches can be made horizontally or vertically. Used to form the nose, satin stitch can be worked into many shapes. When working this stitch, aim for neat and crisp edges. This may be difficult when working over dense seamlines, such as at the muzzle tip.

Your First Bear

T he order of working is the same for all bears. This first bear, called *Algie,* is straightforward to make and is ideal for a beginner's first bear-making project. The pattern pieces are easy to handle and do not require too much stuffing. With his dense fur and charming expression, he is bound to give you the confidence to tackle the other bears in this book. Once you have made this bear, you can apply the same techniques to make any of the other bears in this book. The special instructions for each bear highlight techniques that are specific to each bear. The basic materials listed are needed for all bears. Items specific to each bear such as fabric are listed separately.

Making the Basic Bear

Height 11 in (28 cm)

Basic tools and materials	*Materials for the basic bear*
Squared paper and HB drawing pencil OR enlarged photocopies of the pattern templates	¼ yd (0.25 m) of gold-coloured short-pile mohair
Tracing paper	6-inch (15-cm) square of beige felt
One sheet of white modelling card	Tacking cotton to tone with fabric
2H drawing pencil	All-purpose sewing thread to tone with fabric
Masking tape	One 38-mm hardboard joint
2B drawing pencil	Four 30-mm hardboard joints
Draughting pen or fine waterproof marker	Strong polyester thread or carpet twine to tone with fabric
Tailors' chalk or dressmakers' marker pen	2 oz (50 g) polyester filling
Fine crochet hook or bodkin	1lb (500g) woodwool
Stuffing stick and modelling tools	Scraps of black felt OR two 12-mm black buttons
'Sharps' sewing needle	Two 12-mm black boot-button eyes
Dressmakers' pins and long-shanked 'T' pins	Fine black silk embroidery thread
Long darning needle	
Scissors and pliers	

ENLARGING THE PATTERNS BY PHOTOCOPIER

The basic bear pattern pages should be enlarged by 20 per cent. The easiest way of enlarging the patterns shown on pages 32–3 is to use a photocopier with an enlarging facility. These copiers are found in office supply shops, main libraries and high-street printers. The recommended percentage of enlargement required to reproduce each bear is given on the pattern pages. When you have gained more experience you can alter the percentage to produce a bear of any size. Remember that you will need more fabric for larger bears.

You will need to follow the instructions for the photocopier you are using to obtain the correct size of copy. Photocopy each template page. It may save time to photocopy several bears at a time and to take back up copies of each set of templates for future reference. These can be kept in a large envelope or a suitable folder.

ENLARGING THE PATTERNS WITHOUT A PHOTOCOPIER

The patterns have been drawn out on grids. If you do not have access to a photocopier, you can enlarge the patterns by hand by transferring the template shapes to paper with squares the correct percentage larger than those of the pattern page. Make a mark on your paper where each line crosses a side of a square. Once all these crossing places have been marked, join them to form the outlines of the pattern pieces. An artist's flexible rod can be used to help join the marks smoothly. Trace the squared paper drawings to make card templates.

MAKING THE TEMPLATES

1 Use masking tape to hold the enlarged pattern in position. Place a sheet of tracing paper over this. Using a sharp HB pencil, carefully trace the outline of each shape. Remove the tracing paper and turn it face down over a sheet of modelling card. Hold it in place with two strips of masking tape.

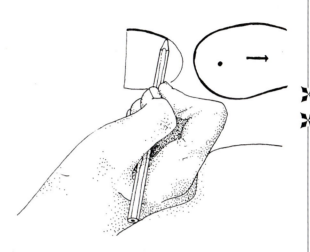

2 Using a sharp 2H pencil, draw over the traced outlines, thus transferring the pattern shapes to the card. When you have completed all the outlines, remove the tracing paper and masking tape. Reinforce the outlines with a fine draughting pen and transfer any pattern markings and instructions to the card. Using craft scissors, cut around each shape as smoothly as possible.

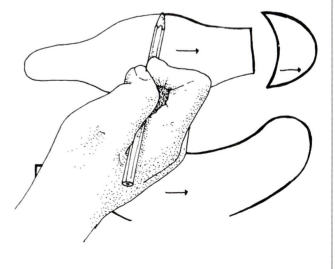

3 *Mark the position of the joints by pushing the point of a pair of scissors through the dot on the template. Later, transfer this marker to your fabric by rotating the sharp point of a pencil through the hole.*

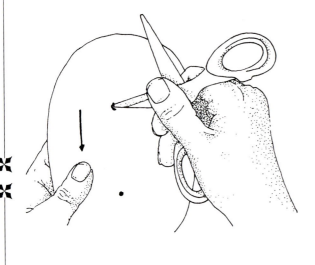

CALCULATING FABRIC REQUIREMENTS

The bears in this book are made from 54-inch (140-cm) wide fabric. If working with a different width, check the length required by drawing your templates on to a sheet of paper of the same width as your fabric. When you have drawn all the shapes, measure the length of paper used. This will gives the amount of fabric required. Keep this drawing; it will provide an excellent layout guide for future use.

TRANSFERRING PATTERN SHAPES TO THE FABRIC

4 *Before transferring pattern shapes to the fabric, it is essential to check the direction of the nap (or pile). This is not necessary when using non-pile fabrics such as cashmere. Simply make sure that the directional arrows on each template match the grain lines. Place the fabric face up. Stroke the pile flat with the palm of your hand, noting in which direction it runs. Turn the fabric over so that the pile runs towards you. Mark this direction with several large arrows, using tailor's chalk or a marker pen.*

5 *Matching the direction of all arrows, place all the templates on to the fabric as close together as possible. While holding the template firmly in place, draw around each shape carefully using a sharp-edged tailor's chalk or marker pen.*

6 *Turn over any template that needs to be used again in reverse, making sure that the directional arrows are still correctly aligned. Draw around the re-positioned templates. Transfer all the pattern markings to the fabric using an HB pencil. If two pairs of pattern pieces are required (as in the case of ears and some arms and legs), draw two, turn over the template and draw a second pair.*

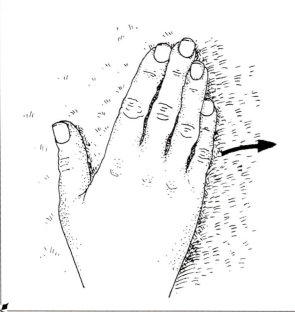

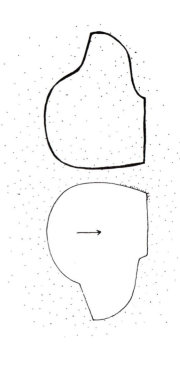

7 Mark the notches for the stuffing openings by sliding the template sideways to show the cutting line. Mark each notch.

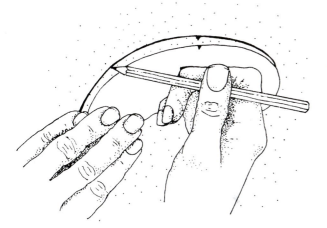

8 Transfer other marks such as dart markers to the fabric by pushing a long-shanked glass-headed pin through the marked point on the template. Ease the template upwards and mark the position before removing the pin. It may be helpful to note the name of the pattern piece and to add pattern details such as 'back neck' to the fabric. Use tailor's tacks to mark any instructions that should appear on the right side of the fabric, such as positions for eyes, noses and ears.

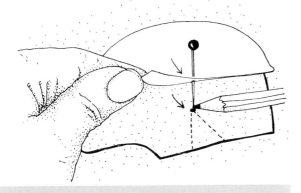

CUTTING OUT PAWS AND PADS

In most cases paws and pads are cut from suedette, felt or leather. When using these fabrics, simply draw around each shape, fitting the templates together as closely as possible. Some velvets have a short nap or pile which will need to be considered when drawing and cutting. Ensure that the nap runs from paw tip to seam on the front paws. Oval foot pads can be cut in either direction, but when assembling the nap should run from toes to heels.

CUTTING THE FABRIC

9 Cut out the pieces using dressmaker's shears or straight-bladed scissors. Take great care when cutting fur fabric not to damage the pile. Push the point of the scissor blade through the fabric on the cutting line. Cut only the ground fabric with a short snipping action. As you cut, gently tease apart the pile. A small amount of shedding will always occur, but try to keep this to a minimum. Put each cut piece into a paper or polythene bag for safe-keeping.

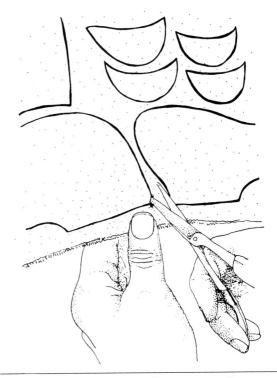

ASSEMBLING THE PATTERN PIECES

10 Place the two side head sections right sides together and pin along the lower muzzle seam, placing the pins at right angles to the edge of the fabric. Pin each paw pad to each inner arm piece, right sides together.

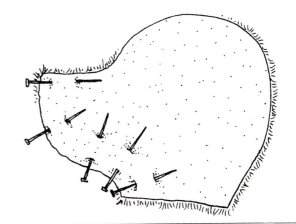

Your First Bear

> **TUCKING IN THE PILE**
> When pinning and tacking fur fabric, use the point of a pin to tuck in the pile as you work. This prevents it from becoming trapped in the seam when machine stitching.

11 *Place body sections right sides together and pin, leaving the seam open between the notches. Some bears in this book have bodies with four sections. In this case pin and stitch in pairs before assembling the whole body.*

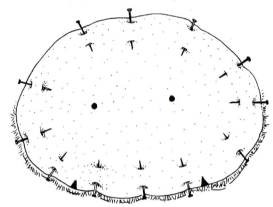

12 *Place the inner and outer legs right sides together in pairs. Pin, leaving the seam open along the lower foot edge and between the notches. Pin both sets of ears right sides together leaving the straight lower edge open.*

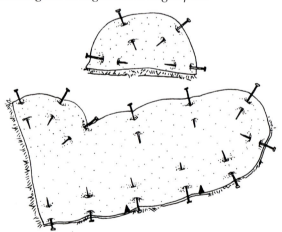

> **SEAM ALLOWANCES**
> On bears 10 to 18 inches (24–46cm) tall the average seam allowance is approximately $^3/_8$ inch (10 mm). Take the smallest seam possible on smaller bears. A seam allowance of $^1/_2$ inch (13 mm) or more can be taken on larger bears.

13 *On each section tack each pinned seam, removing the pins as you work. Do not stitch openings. Adjust the length of the stitches according to the piece being worked. Intricate seams require small, accurate stitches. Machine stitch (or backstitch by hand) all tacked seams, using the reverse facility, if available, to secure the threads at each end. Alternatively, thread cut ends into a needle and oversew by hand with a few small straight stitches to finish. Remove tacking stitches.*

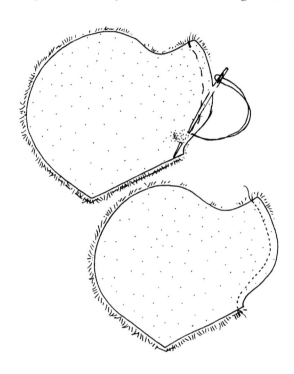

14 *Fit the head gusset between the side head sections and pin, easing the fabric slightly around the forehead and back head curves. Starting from the nose tip, tack each side with small stitches. Remove the pins as you work.*

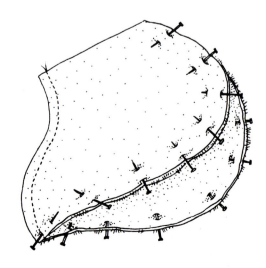

MAKING THE BASIC BEAR

15 Pin the outer and inner arms right sides together, making sure that the paw seams lie flat against the fur fabric. Hold these in position with a few oversewing stitches. Tack along the pinned edges, leaving the seams open between the notches. Remove pins.

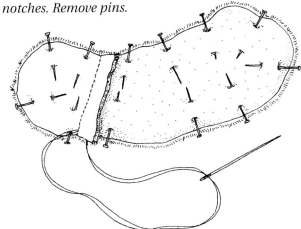

16 Pin each foot pad into each of the lower leg openings. Tack and remove pins. Machine stitch the foot pads by sewing each side of the foot separately, tapering the seam allowance at heel and toe. Close any spaces with a few straight stitches.

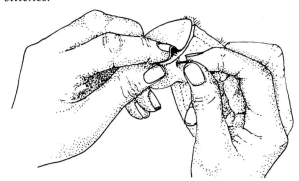

17 Machine stitch the head gusset seam on each side, starting at the neck edge. Close any small gap at the nose tip by hand with a few straight stitches. Trim the muzzle seam to within a few millimetres of the machine stitching.

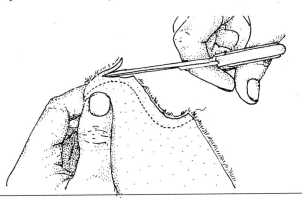

18 Machine stitch all other tacked seams. Remove tacking stitches and turn all sections right sides out. Using a fine steel crochet hook or bodkin, pull out any pile trapped in the stitching. Brush lightly with a brush suitable for the fabric (see page 19).

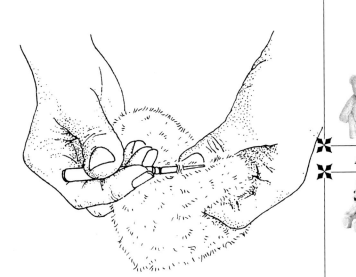

19 Hand sew a line of small straight stitches around each stuffing opening. Use a heavy-duty thread that has been doubled and knotted. Finish with a few oversewing stitches and cut thread.

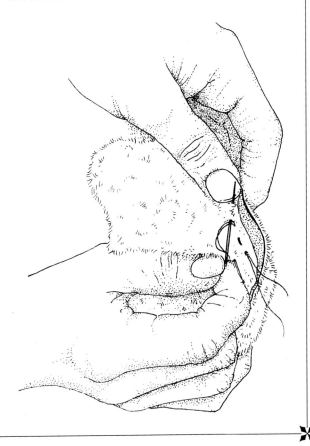

Your First Bear

Stuffing the Bear and Inserting the Joints

20 *Roll a small amount of polyester filling between the palms of your hands to form a small ball. Using a stuffing tool, push this firmly into the nose tip. Continue adding further stuffing until the whole muzzle feels firm and smooth.*

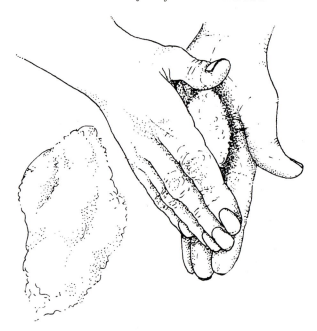

21 *Finish stuffing the head using woodwool. Start at the top of the head and work downwards, pushing a little woodwool into the polyester filling of the muzzle and continuing until the head feels hard and smooth. Pack small balls of filling into any gaps in the seamlines.*

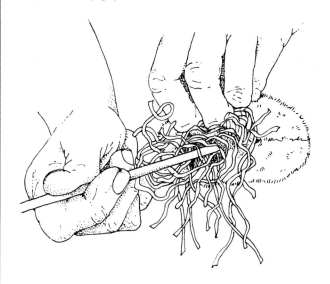

22 *Run a line of tacking stitches around the neck opening, using heavy-duty thread that has been doubled and knotted. Do not cut the thread, but push the point of the needle into the head away from the neck opening until needed again.*

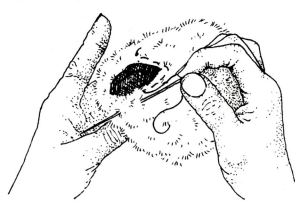

23 *Use the largest hardboard joint for the neck. Thread a washer and a hardboard disc on to the split pin. Push the joint into the neck opening with the split pin protruding.*

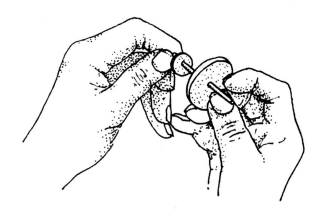

24 *Using the free end of the thread, pull the running stitches up tightly to close the neck opening around the pin. Work long straight stitches backwards and forwards over the joint around the split pin. Pull up firmly and fasten with several oversewing stitches. Cut thread.*

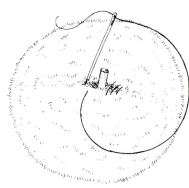

25 *Using a stiletto, make a hole in the seamline of the upper body for the head joint. Ease the threads apart gently, taking care not to weaken the seam or the ground fabric.*

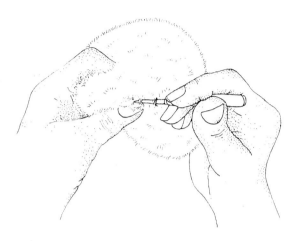

26 *Insert the split pin through the hole. Thread the second hardboard disc and washer onto the split pin inside the body cavity. Using pliers, bend the legs of the split pin over, forcing the discs together as tightly as possible. The curved ends of the pin should push against the washer.*

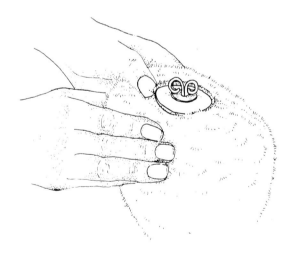

27 *Stuff each paw and foot pad with polyester filling until smooth and firm. Continue stuffing with woodwool until the lower edge of the opening is reached. Using the stiletto and working from the wrong side of the fabric, make a hole at the marked joint placement position. Thread a washer and hardboard disc onto a split pin, insert into the limb.*

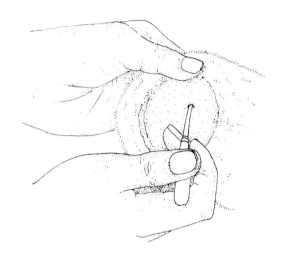

28 *Holding the hardboard disc against the fabric, pack the upper section of each limb with woodwool, completely covering the end of the joint. Continue stuffing the limb until it is firmly packed. Using an upholstery needle, attach a length of heavy-duty thread to one end of the stuffing opening and ladder-stitch closed, pulling the thread up firmly every few stitches. Finish with a few tiny oversewing stitches.*

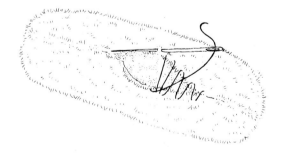

29 *From inside the body, make a hole with the stiletto for each limb at the marked placement points. Attach each limb by inserting the pin through the fabric. Make sure that the limbs are correctly positioned with feet facing frontwards and arms curved forwards. Complete each joint as in step 26.*

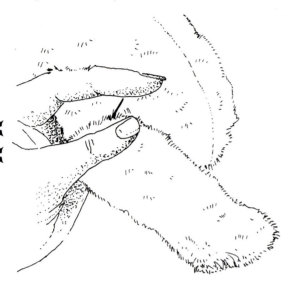

30 *Stuff the body firmly with woodwool, paying special attention to the areas around the joints. Close the stuffing opening with ladder stitch.*

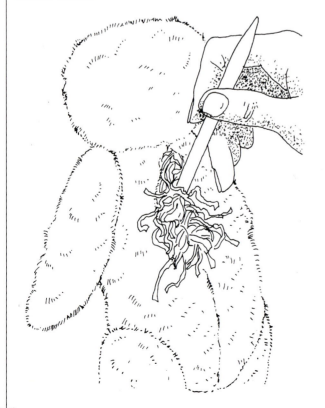

THE EYES

31 *Pin black buttons or circles of black felt in each eye position, so that you can make any adjustments before the eyes are finally applied. The eyes for this bear are set across the head gusset seam line, about 1⅛ in (3 cm) from the nose tip. Thread a long upholstery needle with a doubled and knotted length of carpet twine or heavy-duty thread. You will need sufficient thread to work across the head twice. Take the needle from the first eye position, through the head to the second eye position, bringing the needle out of the fabric and pulling the thread slightly.*

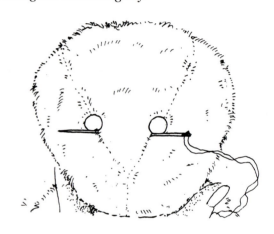

32 *Remove the felt or button marker. Using a stiletto make a small hole around the thread at the second eye position. The hole must be large enough to admit the eye 'bail' or loop. Thread an eye onto the needle, taking the needle back down through the hole and back across the head to the first eye position. Use pliers to gently flatten the 'bail' slightly. Be careful – too much pressure will shatter the glass. Pull the anchoring thread tight, to bring the bail inside the head.*

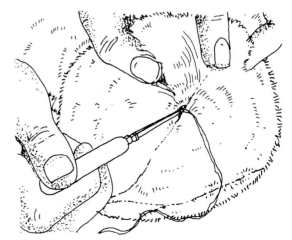

33 Make a hole around the thread in the first eye position. Attach a second eye, flattening the bail as before. Take the thread back through the hole and downwards to the rim of the neck joint, pulling as tightly as possible. Finish with a few small oversewing stitches. Cut threads close to the fabric and brush.

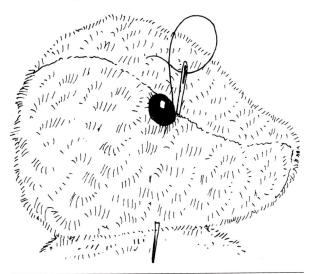

THE EARS

34 Hold the ears in position with several 'T' pins before finally deciding on the position. The ears of this bear are set along the sides of the head with the inner edge across the head gusset and the outer edge 3½ in (9 cm) from the lower edge of the muzzle. Attach a length of heavy-duty thread to the centre point of the inside of the back of one ear and work the outer edge, using small oversewing stitches. These should not be visible on the right side. Make a few extra stitches at the outer edge to secure, fold in excess seam fabric and work back across the ear to the inner edge. Make a few extra holding stitches.

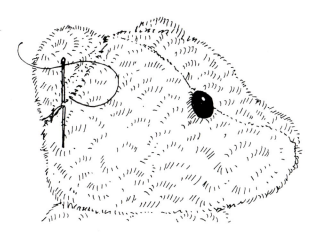

35 Folding in the front edge of the ear, work across the front of the ear, using tiny oversewing stitches and pulling the thread tight as you work. Finish off with several more stitches and cut the thread close to the ground fabric. Pull out any trapped pile using a stiletto or crochet hook and brush lightly. Attach the second ear in the same way.

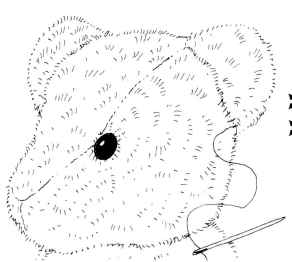

TRIMMING THE MUZZLE

36 Clip long or dense mohair around the muzzle before embroidering. Work slowly with a pair of embroidery scissors, cutting just a little at a time. If necessary, clip the area several times, until you are satisfied with the result.

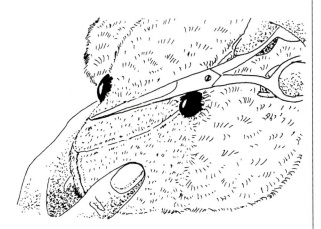

THE NOSE

37 *Thread a 'sharps' needle with a single strand of embroidery silk. Starting from a point high up the muzzle, bring the needle out to one side of the nose tip, pulling until the tail of thread disappears into the head.*

THE MOUTH

39 *Form the mouth by taking a single straight stitch approximately 3½ in (9 mm) in length down the lower muzzle seam.*

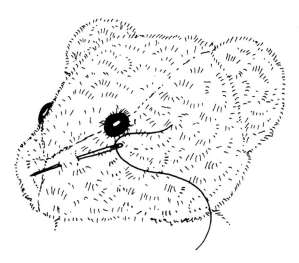

38 *Work a ½-in (13-mm) square of satin stitches horizontally across the nose area. If the ground fabric is very stiff, it may be necessary to use pliers to pull the needle through. Bring the final stitch out at the centre of the base of the nose. Do not cut.*

40 *Work one ½-in (13-mm) straight stitch on each side of the seam to form the mouth. To finish take the needle through the head to a point well away from the muzzle and clip the thread close to the ground fabric.*

THE CLAWS

41 *Using a length of black embroidery thread, work four claws on each paw and pad. Take the needle from a point higher up the limb, and bring it out through the pad (or paw), ready to stitch the first claw. Pull the thread until its tail disappears.*

FINISHING TOUCH

43 *Brush to remove strands of woodwool or filling and take time to admire your new friend.*

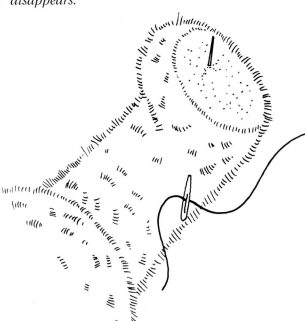

42 *Work a ¾-in (2-cm) straight stitch into the fur fabric just above the seam, bringing the needle out to start the next claw. To finish take the needle through the limb to a point where the thread will be hidden by fur pile. Pull slightly and cut close to the ground fabric.*

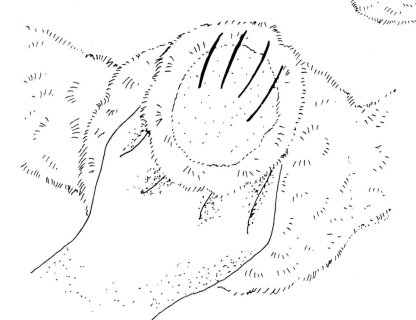

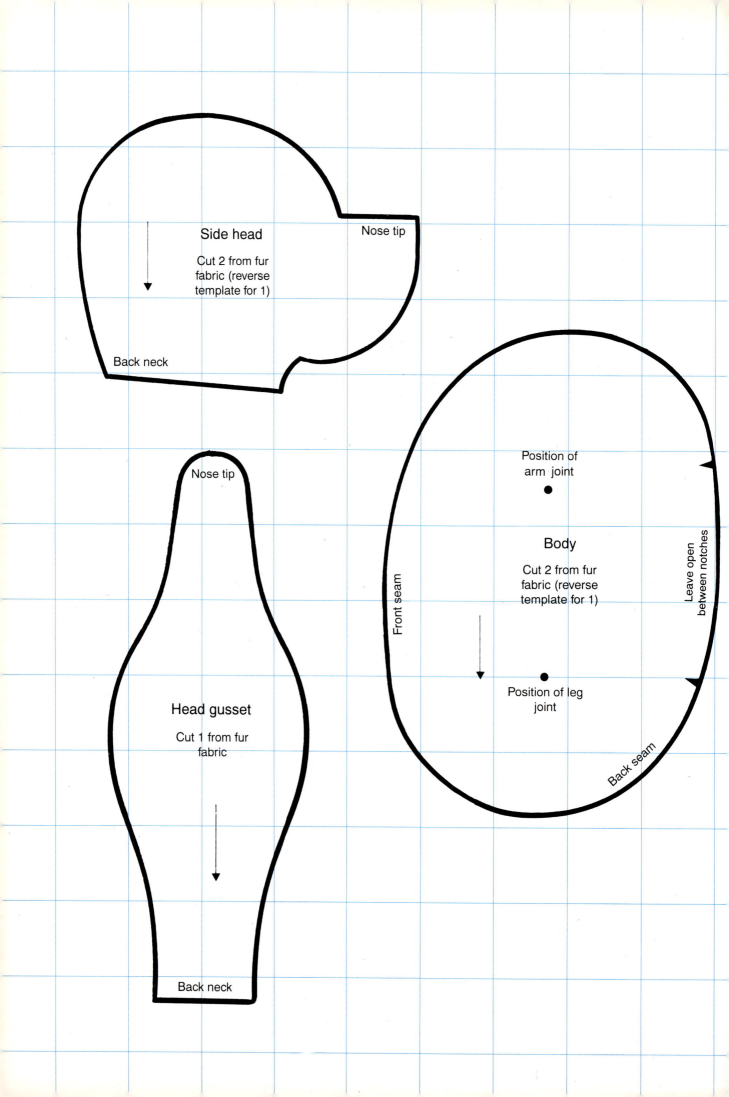

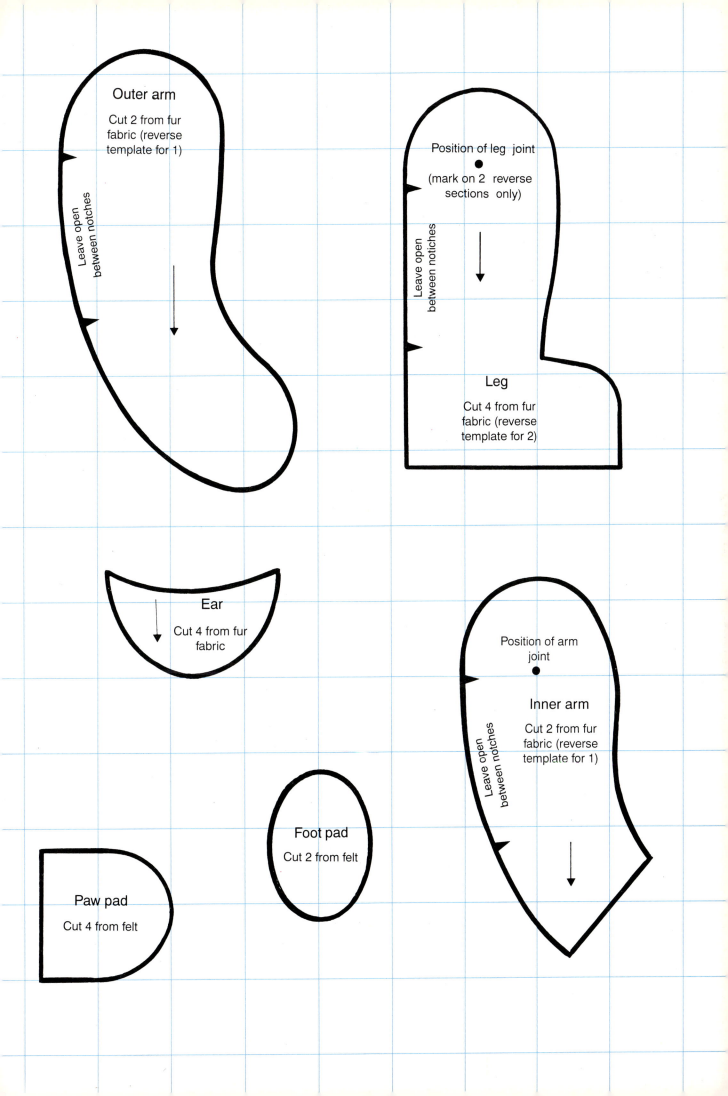

TINY

Height 7 in (18 cm)

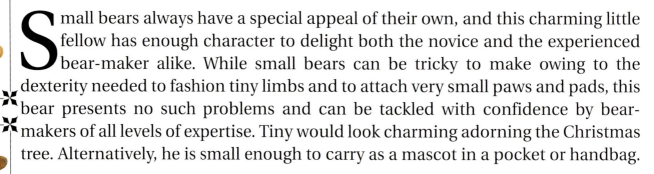

Small bears always have a special appeal of their own, and this charming little fellow has enough character to delight both the novice and the experienced bear-maker alike. While small bears can be tricky to make owing to the dexterity needed to fashion tiny limbs and to attach very small paws and pads, this bear presents no such problems and can be tackled with confidence by bear-makers of all levels of expertise. Tiny would look charming adorning the Christmas tree. Alternatively, he is small enough to carry as a mascot in a pocket or handbag.

Tiny uses an acrylic fabric and an uncomplicated, quick method of construction. The ears, head and body are cut in one piece, and only the arms and legs are jointed. For simplicity, Tiny has no paws or pads. While a modestly priced short-pile acrylic fabric is recommended, he could be worked in mohair or plush to make a tiny companion for a larger bear.

Finding eyes small enough for a miniature bear can be a problem. However, black glass beads often provide the solution. For Tiny black seed beads and spacers have been used. If the hole in the beads is too small to allow the passage of a thin needle and thread, it may be worth trying an old technique. Thread both ends of a hair through the hole in the bead, leaving a loop on one side. Having removed the needle, pass the thread through the looped hair. A gentle pull on the free ends of the hair should bring the loop and the working thread through the hole in the bead. Re-thread the needle and sew the bead into position.

The templates for this bear are reproduced to the correct size to provide a bear approximately 7 in (18 cm) high. You can, of course, reduce or enlarge these templates to make a bear of any size. By reducing the size of the pattern by 60 per cent, you can make a 3-inch (7.5-cm) bear to replace or befriend the fairy on the Christmas tree. Adorn your miniature bear with bow of bright tartan ribbon and sew a loop of dark green thread to the back of his head to enable him to become the centre of attention over the festive season.

Nowadays, mail-order suppliers, particularly in the United States, specialize solely in fabrics and accessories that will enable makers to produce ever smaller and more complex bears. A glance at the pages of specialist teddy bear magazines soon reveals the enormous and growing interest in these delightful miniatures.

35

MINIATURE BEARS

Although 7 in (18 cm) seems to be the upper size limit for most miniature bears, makers past and present have often competed to make the very tiniest of mini bears. For these perfectly formed little creatures, the bear-maker's skill and ingenuity is tested to the full. Often working joints are fashioned from small buttons and strong linen thread. One company, famous for its miniature bears from as early as 1912, was the German firm of Schreyer, trading as Schuco. Unlike its rival Steiff, its reputation was based on a range of coloured bears, including tiny miniatures that measured only 2 inches (5 cm) high.

MATERIALS

In addition to the basic tools and materials listed on page 20, you will also need the following:

¼ yd (0.25 m) caramel short-pile acrylic fabric
Tacking cotton to match fabric
All-purpose sewing thread to tone with fabric
Four 25-mm hardboard joints
Strong polyester thread to tone with fabric
4 oz (100 g) polyester filling

Two circular black glass spacer beads
Two black glass seed beads
'straw' or millinery needle
Black matt cotton embroidery thread
12 in (30 cm) of 7-mm wide pale green single-face satin ribbon

Enlarge the patterns by 20 per cent.

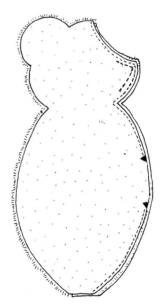

1 One template incorporates the back body, the back head and ears. A second template, which must be cut twice, is used to form the side front body, head and ears. Using a sheet of tracing paper, draw around the template shapes and transfer them to thin card, as described in the basic bear steps 1 and 2.

2 At basic bear step 11, before pinning the fabric shapes together, straight stitch along all sections between the notches. This is important when using a synthetic (knitted) fabric, as it prevents distortion during stuffing. This step is not essential when using a woven fabric such as mohair, which has a much firmer backing.

3 The assembly of the pattern pieces (basic bear, steps 10 – 18) is slightly different. Once cut, place the the two side front sections right sides together. Pin, tack and then stitch along the centre front seam, leaving an opening between the notches. The shape of the head forms the muzzle along this seam. Run a further line of stitching around the muzzle just inside the first row of stitches to reinforce this seam. Once stitched, the seam should be trimmed as close as possible to the first stitching line.

4 To form the ears, head and body, pin the front and back sections right sides together. Stitch around the outline. Turn right sides out and, using the thumb and forefinger, press the ears flat. Machine stitch across the head, following the dotted stitching line shown on the pattern, to define the ears. Sew in thread ends to finish.

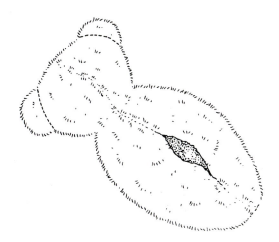

5 The arms and legs are made in the usual manner, omitting basic bear step 16, relating to foot pads. Note that the right and left sides of each leg are cut as a single piece. Only a front seam line is required. Leave a front opening in this seam for stuffing.

6 When stuffing the bear (basic bear, steps 20 – 30), start with the head section and work downwards until the whole body is firmly packed. Pay particular attention to the space between the leg joints. This should be well packed to prevent the split pins from rubbing against each other.

7 At basic bear step 31, the centre point for each beaded eye is ⅝ inch (15 mm) outwards from the tip of the muzzle, in line with the first upper straight stitch of the nose. As the hole in these beads is very small, use a 'straw' needle with two strands of embroidery thread. This should be of sufficient length to stitch the eyes, nose and mouth. Assess and mark the position of the eyes with glass-headed pins. When satisfied, attach the embroidery thread by working several tiny oversewing stitches in the position for the right eye.

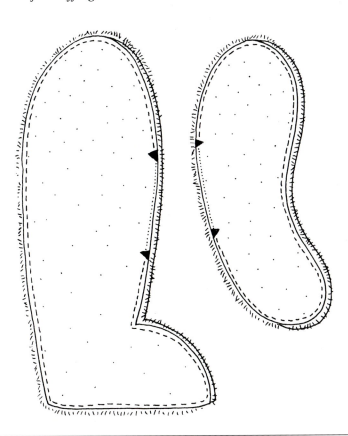

8 *Thread on the spacer bead and then the seed bead. Take the needle and thread back through the spacer bead, and into the fabric at the starting position, across the head, and out at the position of the left eye. Ease the thread through the seed and spacer beads so that the eye sits snugly on the surface of the fabric. Do not attempt to thread the second eye until you are sure that the first eye is correctly sewn. Then thread the spacer and bead for the left eye. Take the thread back through the second hole, adjust the position of the beads and bring the needle out at the muzzle tip. Secure by working several oversewing stitches before using the same thread to embroider the nose and mouth.*

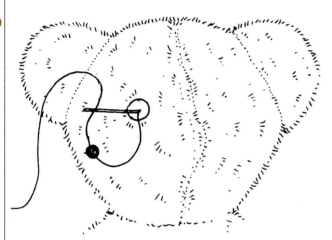

9 *Omit basic bear steps 34 and 35. When you are ready to embroider the nose (basic bear, step 36), trim a small vertical rectangle of fur pile from around the tip of the muzzle. Form the nose from a rectangle of horizontal satin stitches, about ³⁄₈ in by ¹⁄₄ in (10 mm x 6 mm).*

10 *Once you have completed the nose, take a vertical straight stitch (approximately ³⁄₈ in/10 mm) down the lower muzzle seamline. Then take two ¹⁄₄-in (6-mm) straight stitches out to the left and right to form the mouth (basic bear, steps 39 and 40).*

11 *Omit basic bear steps 41 and 42, relating to claws, and brush the completed bear lightly with a nail brush. Finally, tie a length of satin ribbon around the neck. Pull this tightly to accentuate the neck shaping and finish with a smart bow.*

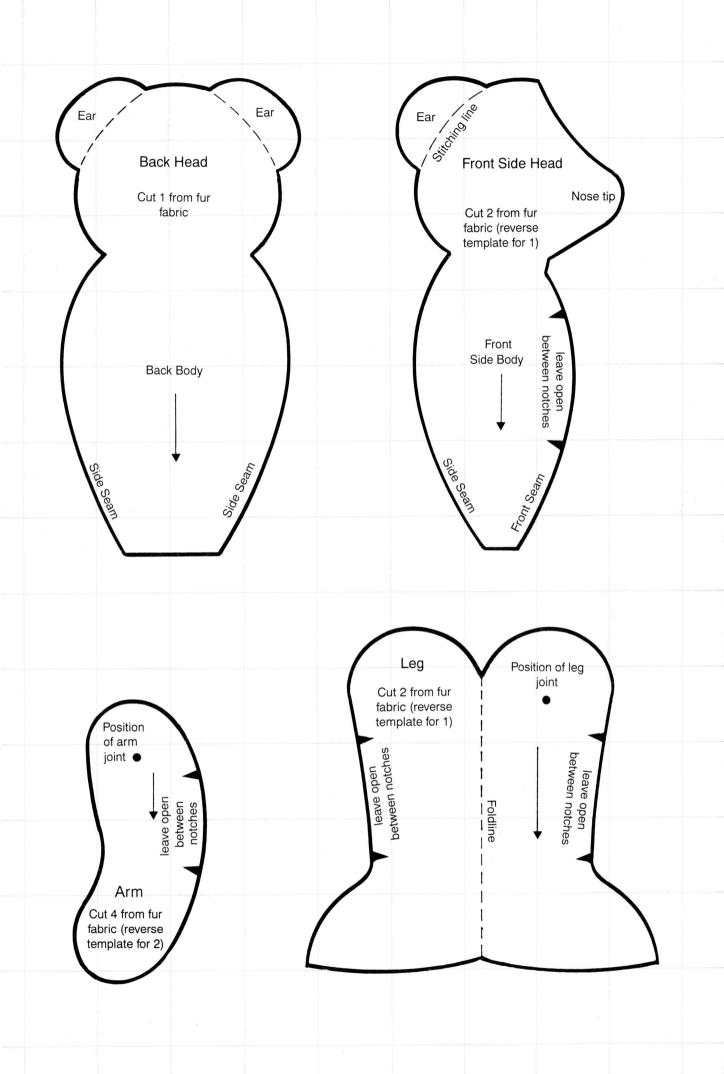

CHARLES
Height 13 in (34 cm)

A traditional bear with modern appeal, Charles has large, oval feet in the classic style and the distinctive long, slim limbs of an early German bear. He is made from 'distressed' long-pile mohair, and is stuffed with a mixture of polyester fibre, sawdust and woodwool. His pads and paws are of light-brown high-quality German felt. Charles has antique-style black boot button eyes and his nose and mouth are embroidered in matt black cotton.

One of the distinguishing features of German and American bears from the early 20th century is the use of small, black boot buttons for eyes. Most modern collectors' bears have black glass eyes, which are held in place by means of a metal 'bail' or loop, through which the anchoring thread is passed. If you intend to use genuine antique boot buttons, bear in mind that to ensure a truly traditional expression they should be smaller than those that would normally be chosen for a modern bear. Like Charles, the best early bears had paws and pads made from the highest quality felt.

Charles is stuffed using a mixture of polyester filling, sawdust and woodwool. In early bears sawdust and woodwool were sometimes mixed in equal quantities. When using sawdust, it is advisable to line each cut piece with calico or curtain lining material to prevent leakage. Although sawdust is a traditional stuffing material, it is not recommended for those suffering from asthma or other allergic respiratory complaints. If you decide to omit the sawdust, substitute an equal weight of woodwool and ignore the instructions relating to the lining.

MATERIALS

In addition to the basic tools and materials listed on page 20, you will also need the following:

½ yd (0.5 m) 'honey' long-pile mohair
½ yd (0.5 m) neutral coloured calico or curtain lining fabric
Tacking cotton to tone with fabric
9-in (25-cm) square of pale-brown felt
All-purpose sewing thread to tone with fabric
One 35-mm hardboard joint

Four 25-mm hardboard joints
Strong polyester thread to match fabric
4 oz (120 g) polyester filling
1 lb (500 g) woodwool
8 oz (250 g) sawdust
Two 10-mm black glass boot-button eyes
Matt-black cotton embroidery thread

Enlarge the patterns by 30 per cent.

Boy and Girl Bears

The star of the late Colonel Bob Henderson's huge collection of bears was a Steiff bear renamed 'Teddy Girl' in later life. Colonel Henderson was a world-famous arctophile (bear lover) and founder of the charity 'Good Bears of the World'. Originally a boy bear, Teddy Girl proved an inspiration for her owner's writing and in later years was the companion of his daughter Cynthia. The bear accompanied the family to the theatre, to restaurants and on holiday. The bear's change of gender occurred in the 1940s when Teddy was put into a dress in time for dinner. The bear was instantly renamed and re-sexed. The enduring charm of this exceptional bear seems to lie in the sweetness of its expression. Bears often seem to display a rather more masculine appeal, resulting, no doubt, from early advertising claims that this was a toy for boys. In general, when clothed, bears do seem more comfortable in sailor suits and heavy sweaters.

Special Instructions

1 When working with long-pile mohair, special care must be taken at the cutting stage (basic bear, step 9). Use small, pointed and very sharp embroidery scissors, and ensure that only the backing fabric is cut. As each piece is finished, carefully tease it free, separating the mohair strands as you do so.

2 Before moving on to basic bear step 10, cut out each pattern piece once again in calico. It is not necessary to line the ears or to cut a separate paw or inner arm. Cut four outer arm sections in calico.

3 Pin each calico piece to the wrong side of its corresponding fur fabric piece. Tack and machine stitch the paw pad and inner arm before attaching the lining fabric. Tack the two layers of each section together using small tacking stitches close to the raw edges. Do not leave open at the stuffing notches. From this point each piece is handled as one. Proceed from basic bear, step 10.

4 At basic bear step 11, before placing the side body sections together, pin the darts along the fold line. Tack and remove pins. Machine stitch along the dart fold line, using the reverse facility on your machine to start and finish. Press the dart towards the back of the body before joining the body sections.

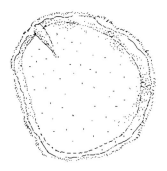

5 At basic bear step 13, leave the tacking stitches around the stuffing openings in place, to prevent distortion of the calico lining during stuffing. Remove all other tacking stitches after the section has been machine stitched and before it is turned. Continue to follow the basic bear instructions until the stuffing stage.

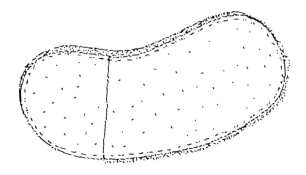
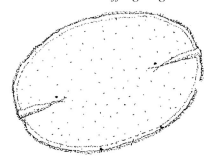

6 At basic bear step 21, if you are using woodwool and sawdust, mix these together before beginning to stuff the bear. Stuff the muzzle, paws and pads of the bear with polyester filling in the normal manner.

7 At basic bear step 31, the eyes should be positioned on each of the head gusset seams about 1 1/4 in (3.5 cm) along from the nose tip.

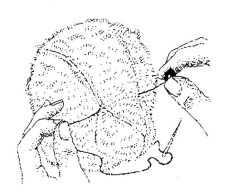

8 At basic bear step 34, position the ears so that the inside edge just crosses the head gusset seam about 2 in (5 cm) from the eyes.

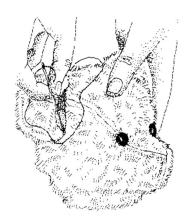

9 Trim the muzzle in an oval shape (basic bear, step 36) before stitching the nose and mouth. Leave the fur long around the eyes.

10 At basic bear step 38, work the nose horizontally in satin stitch using three strands of matt black cotton embroidery thread to form a blunt-pointed triangle. It may be necessary to fill in gaps that become apparent once the triangle is completed, by inserting extra satin stitches between those already worked.

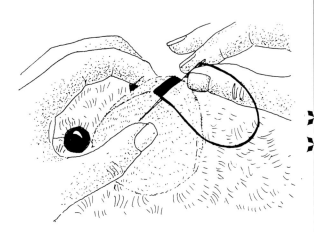

11 Continue with basic bear steps 39 and 40. Form the mouth using six strands of thread. Make a 1/2-in (13-mm) vertical stitch down the lower muzzle seam. Give Charles a wistful smile by positioning the corners of his mouth higher than its centre. Charles has no claws, so omit basic bear, steps 41 and 42.

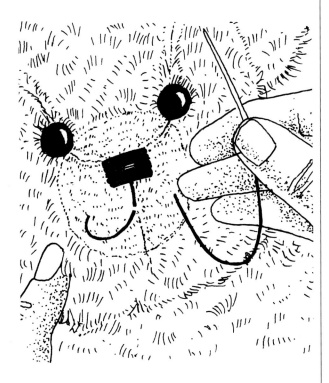

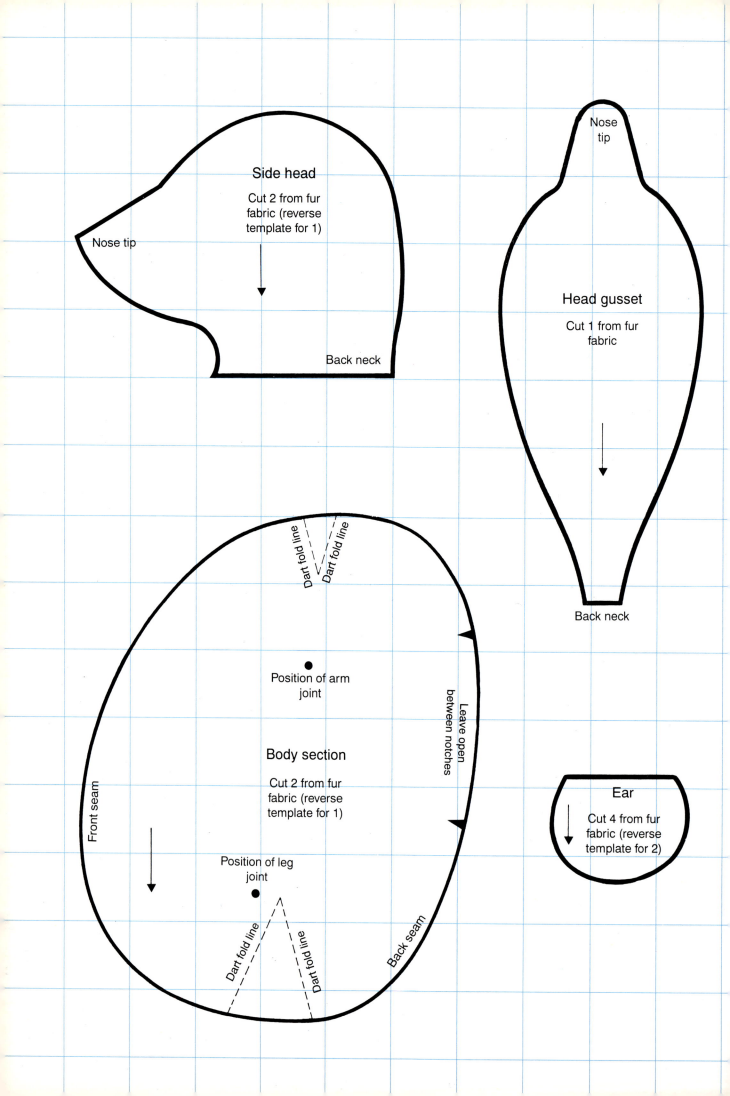

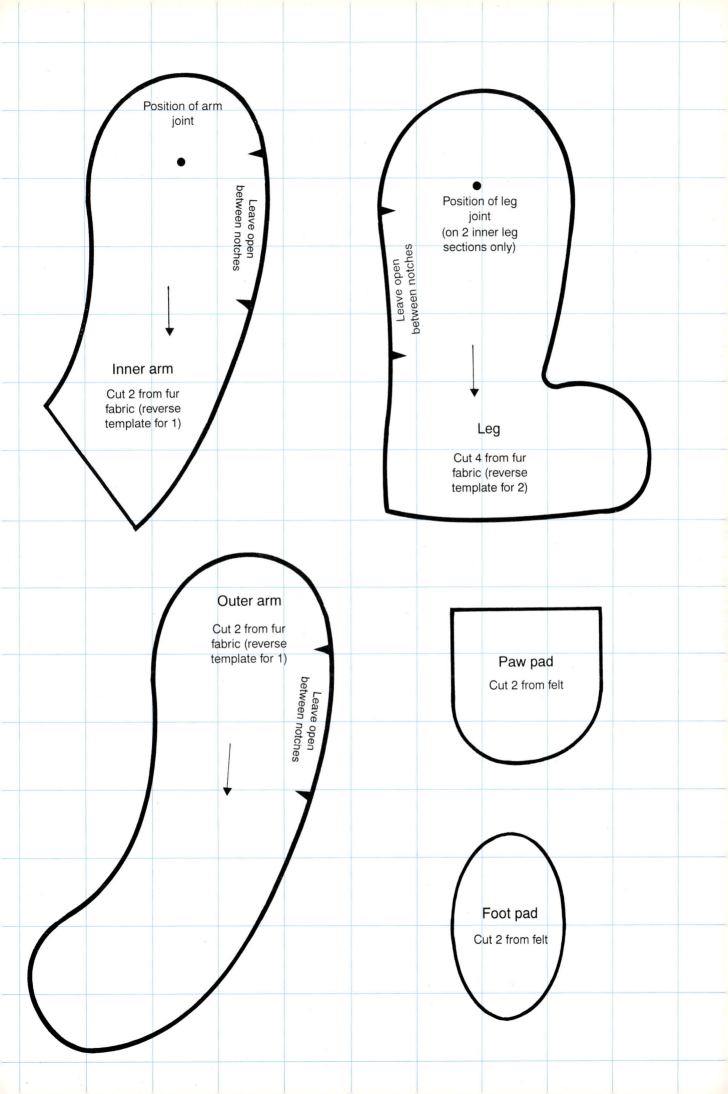

CLAUDE
Height 18 in (46 cm)

Why not take advantage of the new 'out of the attic' range of distressed-pile mohairs, to make this charming, old-fashioned bear. With his long muzzle and distinctive hump, Claude has the look of an instant heirloom. 'Out of the attic' mohair is designed to reproduce the slightly threadbare fur of an original Edwardian bear. Firmly stuffed with woodwool, Claude is a truly traditional bear.

When designing your own bears, one of the most important decisions is how to embroider the nose. Indeed, bear artists the world over are continually searching for unusual shapes and styles, hoping by this means to set their own bears above the competition. There are, of course, many different combinations of angle and length of stitch that can be used to create an appealing nose. In Claude's case, the nose was worked in three stages, using straight stitches set at differing angles. This forms a slightly raised effect.

Make a point of studying the noses of any venerable bears you encounter in specialist museums, shops and toy collections. You will see that individual manufacturers often addressed the problem in distinctive ways. When working on your own bears, you will also find that any variation to such a prominent feature will almost certainly alter the expression and characteristics of your bear. Take the time to experiment with a variety of styles before settling on your final choice. And have the courage and patience to unpick any stitching that does not give the desired result. Until you have developed your confidence, use the centre gusset seams as a guideline for stitching.

MATERIALS

In addition to the basic tools and materials listed on page 20, you will also need the following:

½ yd (0.5m) brown 15 mm distressed-pile mohair
9-in (25-cm) square of brown suede
All-purpose sewing thread to tone with fabric
One 65-mm hardboard joint
Four 50-mm hardboard joints
Heavy-duty polyester thread to tone with fabric

4 oz (120 g) polyester filling
1 lb (500 g) woodwool
Two 15-mm black glass boot-button eyes
High gloss medium black or dark brown embroidery silk
Heavy-duty matt black silk embroidery thread

Enlarge the pattern pieces by 40 per cent.

CLAUDE

BEAR SHAPES

The pattern for Claude is inspired by the design of the early German bears with their slim bodies and definite padded humps. These first bears were based on real bears, which could be seen at that time in many zoos across Europe. It is believed that Margarete Steiff's nephew, Richard, sketched the bears in Stuttgart Zoo before developing the prototype bear known as Friend Petz, which was exhibited at the Leipzig Toy Fair in 1903.

Early bears also had long, thin arms that reached to the knees when standing upright. The arms of most bears of this period were sharply angled to form a wrist and have clearly embroidered claws. Firmly stuffed with woodwool, these bears were quite unlike today's mass produced cuddly bears.

SPECIAL INSTRUCTIONS

1 Make templates and cut out the fur fabric in the usual manner (basic bear, steps 1 – 7). The pads and paws are cut from suede. Place the suede right sides down on a flat surface and draw around each template once. Turn each template over and draw around them a second time. A sharp lead pencil or non-smudge draughting pen is best for this. Cut out each shape carefully. Fine suede has a tendency to slip, so use sharp, pointed scissors and cut a little at a time.

2 At basic bear step 10, pin and tack the pads and paws in the usual way, but limit the number of pins and stitches required to hold the shapes securely – the fewer holes in the suede the better. If you encounter any difficulty in pulling through the needle, try using a pair of pliers for extra purchase.

3 Claude's body has four sections. At basic bear step 13, pin and stitch the two front sections and the two back sections together before assembling the whole body.

4 At basic bear step 13, before sewing the pads and paws, change your machine needle to a three-sided 'leather' needle. This will make stitching easier, and will prevent damage to the suede. Remember to change back to your usual needle before sewing fur fabric again.

5 At basic bear step 25, push the head pin through the intersection of the seamlines at the top of the body. Assemble the joint and stuff the limbs as usual.

6 At basic bear step 29, measure down each side seam line approximately 1 1/2 – 2 in (4 – 5 cm) and, using a stiletto or bodkin, make a small hole to allow for the insertion of the arm pins. The position of the hole for each leg pin is about 2 3/4 in (6 – 7 cm) up from the lower body seam intersection. Complete the stuffing.

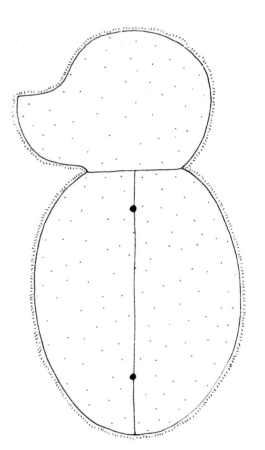

7 At basic bear step 31, place the eyes on the side seams of the head gusset, approximately 2 in (5 cm) from the nose tip. The fur fabric around the eyes can be trimmed back a little if necessary, depending on the length of the pile.

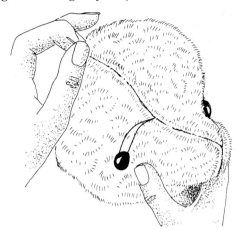

8 At basic bear step 34, set each ear so that its upper edge sits on the head gusset side seam about 2 ¾ in (7 cm) from the eye. The lower edge of each ear is approximately 4 ¾ in (12 cm) from the nose tip.

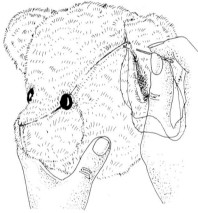

9 Continue until basic bear step 36. Trim the muzzle back to the point where the face begins to broaden and flatten out – about 2 in (5 cm) from the nose tip.

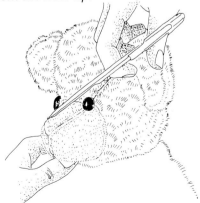

10 Begin stitching the nose (basic bear, steps 37 and 38) by embroidering a kite-shaped triangle. Make several straight stitches to either side of the lower muzzle seam. These straight stitches should become progressively shorter as the tip of the muzzle is reached. Finish off with 8 – 10 straight stitches across the bridge of the nose. This will give a slightly raised effect. The completed nose should measure ⅝ in (15 mm) across and ¾ in (20 mm) deep.

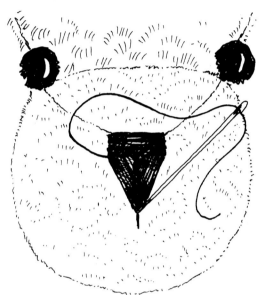

11 Continue to embroider the mouth (basic bear, steps 39 and 40) by taking a straight stitch measuring approximately ½ in (13 mm) downwards along the lower muzzle seam. Form the mouth by taking one horizontal straight stitch to left and right of this vertical stitch. Each stitch should measure approximately ⅝ in (18 mm). To finish, sew the claws in heavy-duty black silk thread (basic bear, steps 41 and 42).

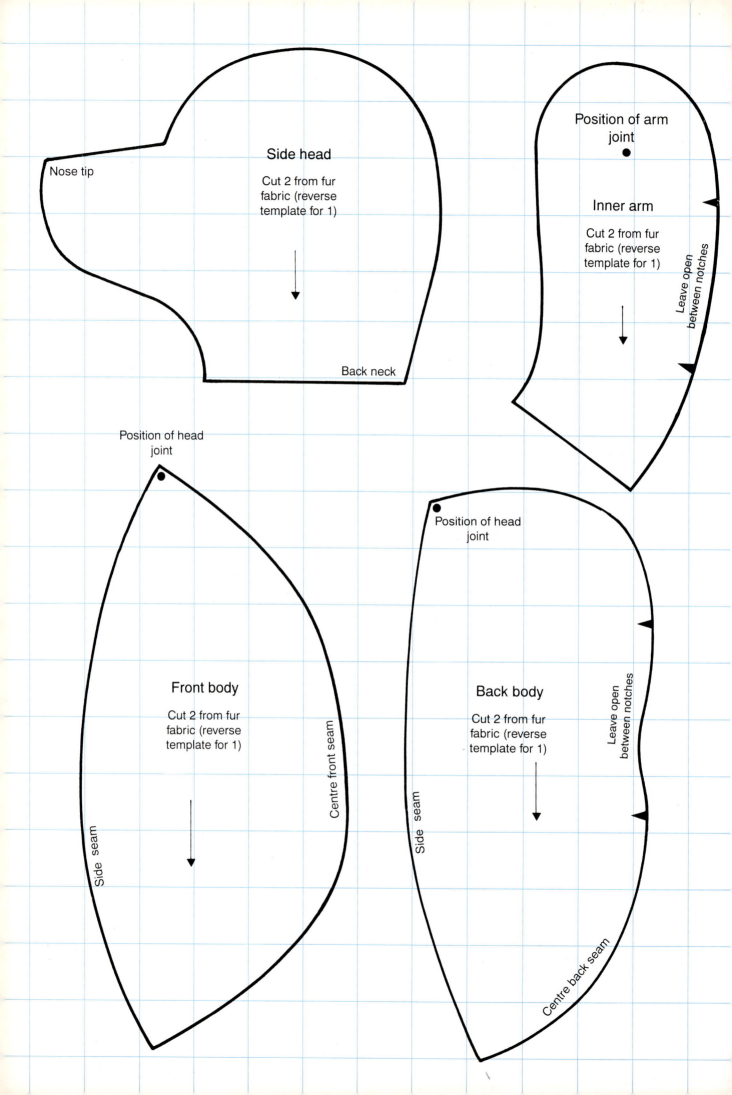

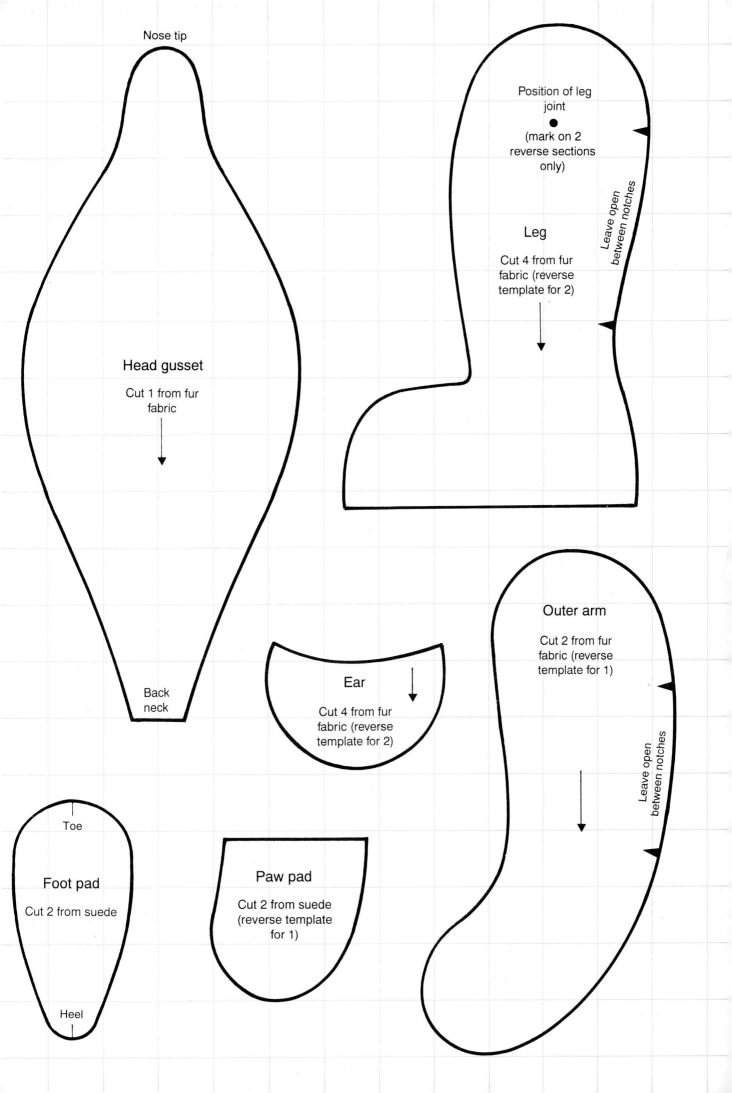

ASTBURY

Height 11 in (28 cm)

This appealing small bear is made from a very long-pile mohair in a pale honey colour. This fabric would normally be used for a larger bear, but it gives *Astbury* a special 'urchin' look that, along with his twinkling black eyes, makes him a truly charming companion.

Do not be nervous of tackling patterns using long-pile mohair. Although great care must be taken when cutting the backing fabric to avoid cutting the fur pile, any small errors of judgement that might result in a bald seamline on a bear made with a short-pile mohair, can be covered by brushing up the surrounding long pile to hide these mistakes. In addition, if you are not very confident when sewing in foot pads or attaching ears, minor mistakes and inaccuracies can again be covered by a longer pile. While experienced bear-makers will enjoy the challenge of working with a longer pile, beginners should be encouraged by the results obtained by making this bear, which should inspire confidence in yourself and praise from your friends.

Astbury is pictured on the facing page with *Prudence*, a bear made from the same pattern in a fabric of a darker colour.

MATERIALS

In addition to the basic tools and materials listed on page 20, you will also need the following:

¼ yd (0.25 m) pale honey 1-in (25-mm) pile mohair
6-in (15-cm) square of beige felt
Tacking cotton to tone with fabric
All-purpose sewing thread to tone with fabric
One 50-mm hardboard joint
Four 36-mm hardboard joints

Strong polyester thread or carpet twine to tone with fabric
2 oz (50 g) polyester filling
1 lb (500 g) woodwool
Scraps of black felt OR two 10-mm black buttons
Two 10-mm black boot-button eyes
Fine black silk embroidery thread

Enlarge the pattern pages by 20 per cent.

Bear Noses, Past and Present

The traditional method for creating a bear nose is by embroidering it in dark brown or black cotton or silk embroidery thread. The shape of nose is determined by the expression required and the wrong choice can easily spoil his character. The simplest and quickest method is to make a square or rectangle of straight stitches, but other shapes, including oval, round or fan-shaped, can suit certain bears.

During the 1920s moulded snouts of gutta percha and rubber were introduced and proved popular. However, a truly classic bear should be provided with a hand-made nose in a style that has been chosen to reflect his particular personality.

A useful tip when undoing a wrongly worked nose is to slip one blade of your embroidery scissors behind the stitches and cut through them all. These can then be pulled out singly using a pair of pliers or tweezers.

Special instructions

1 Follow the instructions for the basic bear, but when working steps that refer to machine sewing, take care to tease out any pile trapped in the stitching as each seam is sewn.

2 At basic bear step 31, place each eye on the head gusset seam, with its centre about 1 ¼ in (3 cm) from the tip of the muzzle.

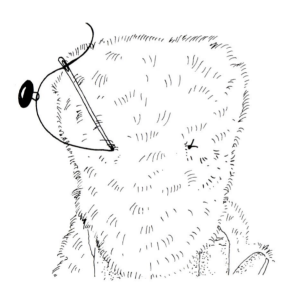

3 Set the ears (basic bear, step 34) across the sides of the head, so that the inner third lies across the head gusset and the outer tip is about 2 in (5 cm) from the lower edge of the muzzle.

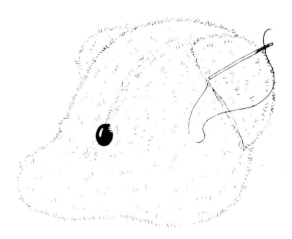

4 At basic bear step 36, trim back the fur pile around the muzzle and eyes, about 1 ½ in (4 cm) from the tip of the muzzle to form an oval.

5 Form the nose (basic bear, steps 37 and 38) by embroidering a ½-in (13-mm) square. Use a single strand of fine black silk embroidery thread. Position the nose across the lower muzzle seam, just below the tip of the head gusset.

7 At basic bear steps 41 and 42, embroider four ¾-in (2-cm) claws on each pad and paw, using a single strand of fine silk thread.

6 For the mouth (basic bear, steps 39 and 40), make a ⅜-in (10-mm) straight stitch downwards along the lower muzzle seam. Then take two ½-in (13-mm) straight stitches outwards to form the mouth.

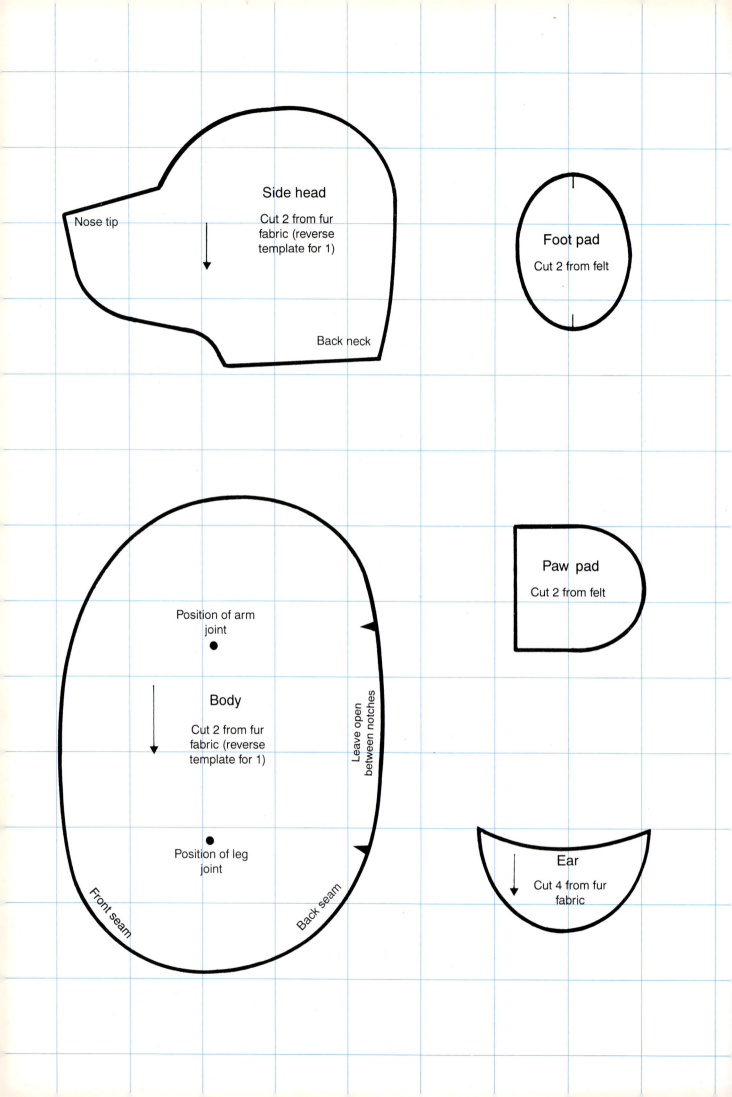

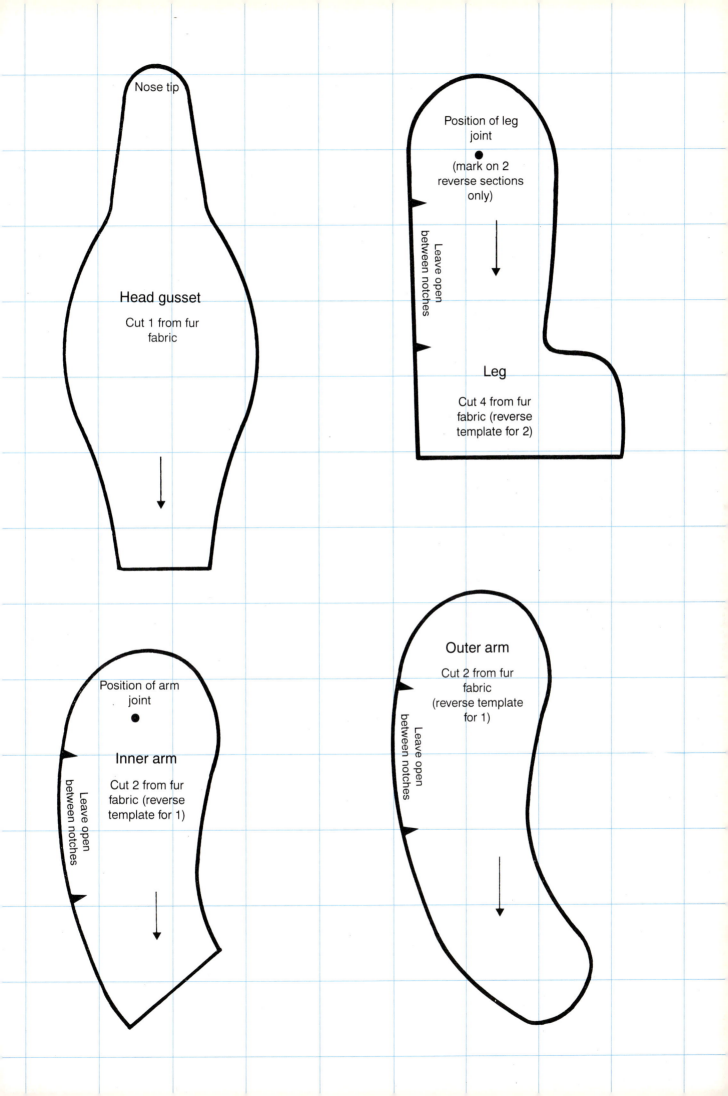

LITTLE ROGER

Height 16 in (41 cm)

This thoughtful and dependable bear has been made using a dense-pile ivory mohair. Little Roger's paws and pads are cut from light cream felt and his long muzzle is lightly trimmed around his bright eyes and tiny nose to accentuate his unusual features.

White mohair in a variety of finishes can be used to make distinctive bears from any of the patterns in this book. Some white mohair fabrics are very loosely woven. This can make sewing difficult, so take this into consideration when planning any project. Check the stability of your fabric by brushing it lightly or gently pulling at the pile. If too many strands are shed, it may be wise to choose a stronger material.

Special care must be taken when working with white and pastel shades to keep the fabric clean. Mark only the basic pattern instructions, using a chalk pencil that can easily be brushed out. Ink can seep through the ground fabric, leaving an unsightly stain on your bear. All cut pieces should be kept wrapped in a clean pillowcase or tea towel when not in use and while working it is useful to keep a clean cloth over your knees. This will prevent too many white hairs attaching themselves to your clothes and will also safeguard the delicate fabric.

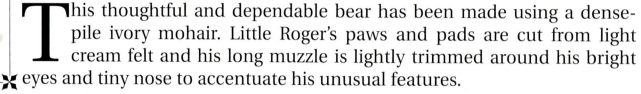

The construction of Little Roger's muzzle is slightly unusual. The head gusset is much longer than for most of the bears in the book and does not finish at the nose tip. Instead, it curves around the side head, tapering to a point in the lower muzzle seam. The fur pile is then trimmed back along the gusset, using the seam lines as a guide. By widening the head gusset slightly, you can easily adapt this pattern to produce your own individual and distinctive bear.

MATERIALS

In addition to the basic tools and materials listed on page 20, you will also need the following:

¼ yd (0.25 m) of ivory long, dense-pile mohair
Tacking cotton to tone with fabric
10-in (25-cm) square of cream felt
All-purpose sewing cotton to tone with fabric
One 65-mm hardboard joint

Four 50-mm hardboard joints
Heavy-duty polyester thread to tone with fabric
4 oz (100 g) polyester filling
1 lb (500 g) woodwool
Two 16-mm brown glass eyes with black pupils
Black high-gloss fine embroidery silk

Enlarge the pattern pages by 30 per cent.

WHITE BEARS

The first white bears were made during the early 1900s. In 1921 the English firm of Chad Valley printed a catalogue of bears described as the 'most lifelike toys ever produced'. Among these were bears made from a fabric described as 'London' white fur. However, white bears did not achieve wide popularity until the 1950s, when London Zoo's polar bear, Ivy, gave birth to her son, Brumas. The arrival of this little fellow caught the public imagination and sales of white bears soared.

Another famous white bear is, of course, Rupert, the comic strip creation of the artist Mary Tourtel, who worked for the Daily Express in 1920. Rupert stories have enchanted children in many different countries to the present day. Early Rupert annuals are eagerly sought by collectors the world over, and in good condition these command high prices.

SPECIAL INSTRUCTIONS

1 Follow the instructions for the basic bear to step 14, omitting step 10. Little Roger's head gusset differs slightly from that of the basic bear, in that it does not finish at the nose tip, but continues along the lower muzzle. Pin the side head sections to the head gusset, matching the placement notches on either side. Carefully ease the fabric around and under the nose tip. Tack this securely to prevent puckering or slipping when the seam is stitched. Once both sides of the head gusset are machine stitched, pin, tack and stitch the remaining lower muzzle seam. Trim any excess fabric from the stitching before turning the head. Continue from basic bear step 15.

2 At basic bear step 31, place the eyes so that they lie on each of the head gusset seams about 2 in (5 cm) from the nose tip.

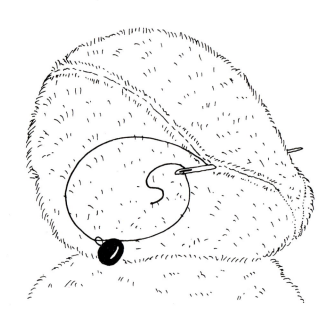

3 At basic bear step 34, stuff the ears slightly with a little polyester filling before attaching them. Push the filling well into the top of the ear when sewing to prevent strands from becoming trapped in the oversewing stitches. Then attach the ears as usual (basic bear, steps 34 and 35). The ears should be placed at the side of the head, their top edges just touching the gusset seams approximately 5 ¾ in (14.5 cm) from the nose tip. The lower edge of the ear should sit 4 ½ in (11.5 cm) from the tip of the nose.

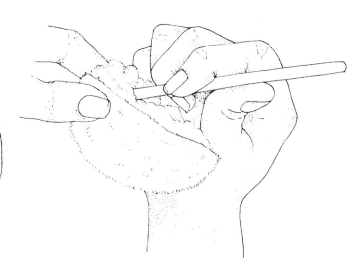

4 At basic bear step 36, lightly trim the fur back on the top of the muzzle along the head gusset. Then, starting at the nose tip and working downwards along the lower muzzle gusset, trim the fur back to the ground fabric, finishing in a point at the tip of the lower gusset.

6 To form the mouth (basic bear, steps 39 and 40), using a single strand of embroidery silk, take a ³⁄₈ in (1 cm) straight stitch downwards from the centre point of the lower edge of the nose. Then take a straight stitch to either side to form a wide 'Y' shape. Each arm of the 'Y' should measure approximately ³⁄₈ in (1 cm).

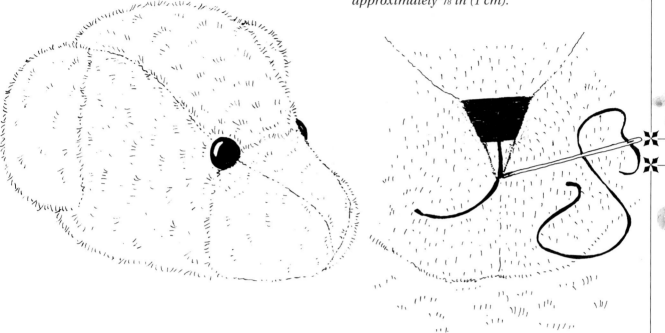

5 Continue with basic bear steps 37 and 38. Using one strand of embroidery silk, embroider the nose in a small rectangle that extends across the lower muzzle gusset from seam to seam to a depth of ³⁄₈ in (1 cm). Work straight stitches across the seam until the nose is well covered. Trim any stray strands of mohair with

7 This bear has no embroidered claws, so omit basic bear steps 41 and 42 and complete by lightly brushing the fur of the muzzle and checking that your trimming is accurate. Where necessary trim back any longer strands of mohair, being careful not to disturb your embroidery stitches.

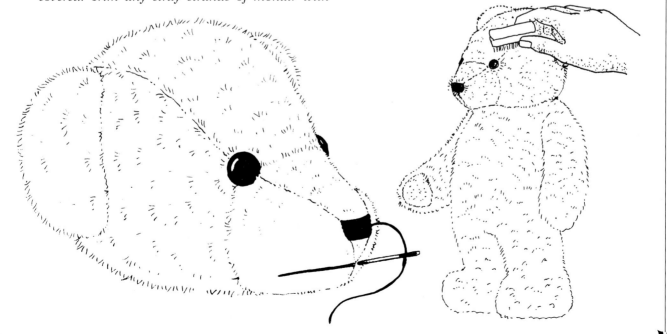

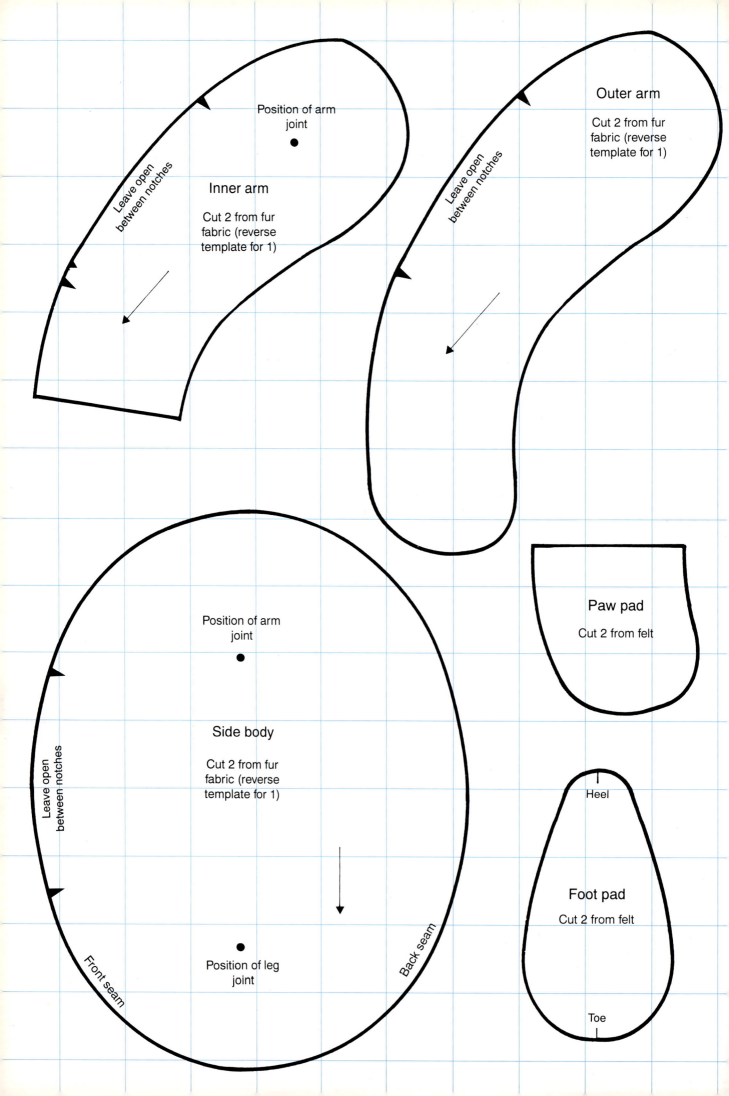

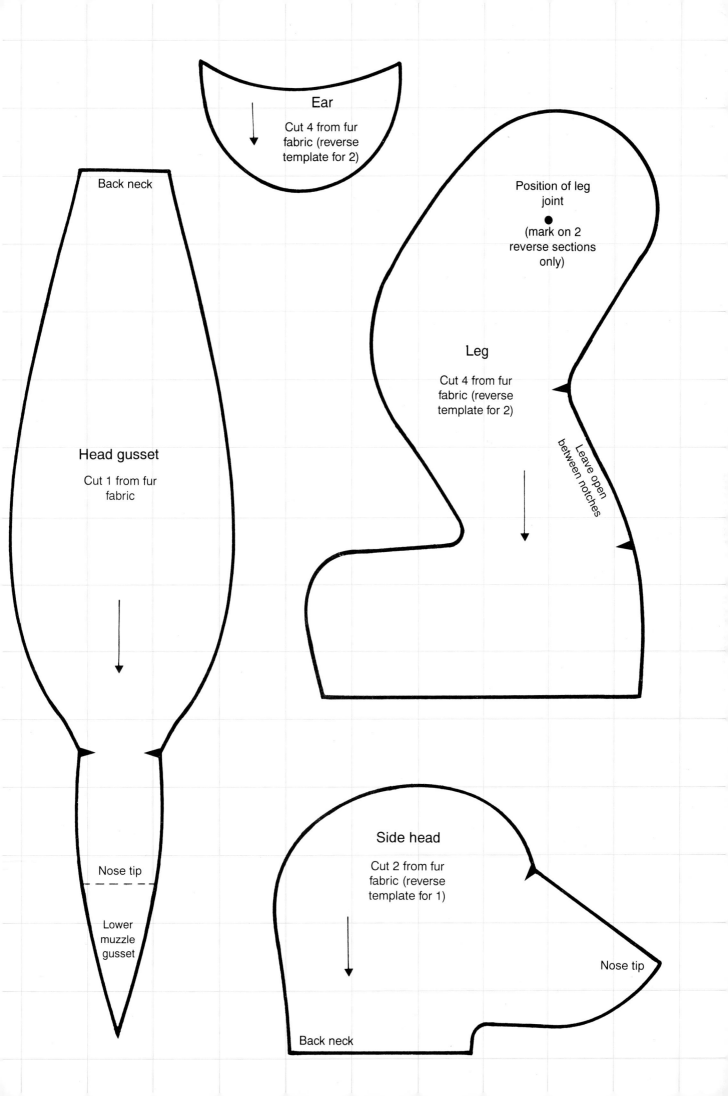

BERTIE

Height 20 in (51 cm)

T his lovable bear has limbs filled with plastic pellets, giving him a relaxed feel. Made from caramel-coloured feather-pile mohair, he combines traditional quality with a modern short-muzzled face. His pads and paws are cut from terracotta upholstery velvet and his claws are embroidered with a dark brownish-red embroidery thread.

The ruffled look of this long-pile fabric creates a bear with a charming ragamuffin appeal. One of a new and exciting range of materials, it is ideal for the bear-maker who wants to try something different.

Bertie's nose is one of his distinctive features. The technique used here is ideal for those who are not confident of their embroidery skills. A circle of fabric – in this instance, cashmere, is stitched and stuffed to make a raised, 'button' nose that is slip-stitched into position. The cheeky expression this creates is just right for a modern bear, who is well aware of the impression he is making.

MATERIALS

In addition to the basic tools and materials listed on page 20,
you will also need the following:

½ yd (0.5 m) of caramel feather-pile mohair
Tacking cotton to match fabric
⅛ yd (12 cm) of terracotta upholstery velvet
All-purpose sewing thread to tone with fabric
and in black
Scrap of black fine non-pile fabric
(wool, cashmere or felt)
Three 50-mm hardboard joints

Two 35-mm hardboard joints
Heavy-duty polyester thread to match fabric
1 lb (500 g) polyester filling
8 oz (250 g) plastic pellets
Funnel with a wide, short tube
Two 14-mm black boot button eyes
Medium-weight black embroidery silk
Dark terracotta embroidery thread

Enlarge the pattern pages by 40 per cent.

> **BEAR FABRICS**
> The search for exciting, experimental fabrics has always occupied makers of quality bears, and fabric manufacturers have endeavoured to meet this demand. During the 1920s, soft-toy making was revolutionized by the introduction of rayon plush, an artificial silk fabric that had been developed for the furniture industry. This fabric could be dyed using chemical processes, producing a wide range of strong, bright colours that can be seen in bears of the period.

Special Instructions

1 Follow the instructions for the basic bear to step 9, but before assembling the head (step 10), make the darts in the side head sections. Do not slash, but hold down with your thumb and finger towards the back of the head when tacking. Stay stitch these flat with a few oversewing stitches before machine stitching. At basic bear step 11, pin and tack the body section in the same way before joining the two pieces.

2 At basic bear step 27, stuff the paws and pads with polyester filling, pushing this firmly into position with a stuffing stick. Then insert the hardboard joints. Use 50-mm joints for the legs and 35-mm joints for the arms. You will probably find that they are quite a tight fit, and you may need to force them into position. Try wriggling the joint backwards and forwards until in place.

3 At basic bear step 31, before completing the stuffing of the limbs, take a small amount of polyester filling and pack this around each joint head, so that it is completely covered.

4 To stuff each limb, insert the tip of the funnel into the opening and tip in the pellets a little at a time. Hold the tube tip away from the surface of the pellets already in place and from time to time, push these further into the arm or leg, settling them against the polyester filling. As you complete each section, ladder stitch the opening closed a little at a time to prevent the pellets pushing out. In this way, you should have just enough room to insert the nozzle for the addition of the final few pellets. The amount of pellets required to fill each section is a matter of choice and depends on how relaxed you want the limbs to be. Because of the fluid nature of the pellets, you will not achieve a firm fill. If you prefer this, substitute extra polyester filling for the pellets. Stuff the body as for the basic bear.

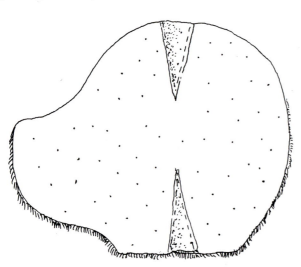

5 At basic bear step 31, place the eyes about 1 1/2 in (4 cm) from the nose tip across each head gusset seam. You may wish to open up the eyes by carefully clipping away any covering pile. Continue until you have completed basic bear step 33.

7 At basic bear step 36, trim the pile around the nose tip and the front edge of the muzzle, graduating your clipping so that no definite line is produced. Clip a little around the eyes.

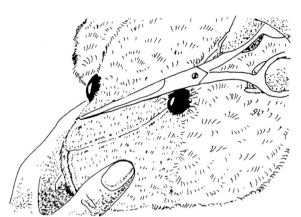

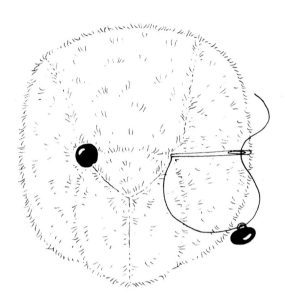

8 Instead of embroidering the nose (basic bear steps 37 and 38), cut a circle of black non-pile fabric approximately 2 in (5 cm) in diameter. Using a length of knotted black sewing thread, run a line of tiny straight stitches around the outer edge of the circle. Do not fasten off, but push a small ball of polyester filling into the centre of the circle, pulling up the running stitches slightly as you do so. Tuck all the filling neatly into the little bag you have made and check that you have used sufficient to make a plump round nose tip. When you are happy with the result, pull the threads up tightly and close with a few oversewing stitches.

6 At basic bear step 34, place the inner edge of each ear on the gusset seam. When placing the ears, curve them slightly so that they slope forwards a little. The lower edge of the ear should be above the muzzle line about 4 in (10 cm) from the point of the muzzle. Stitch carefully in place. The density of the pile may make this difficult, so use your needle to push the strands out of the way as you work.

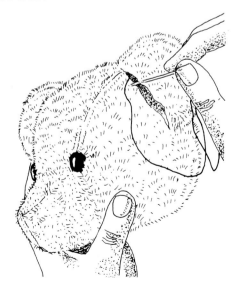

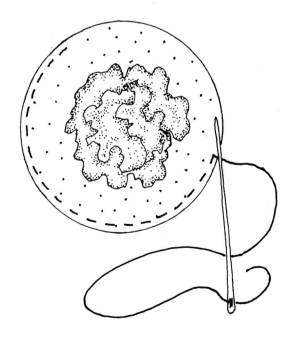

9 *Place the nose tip in position at the end of the muzzle, so that when pressed against the point of the nose it lies just over the tip and extends down along the lower muzzle seam. Using the attached needle and thread, sew the nose into position using tiny, invisible oversewing stitches. Pull the thread tightly and, if necessary, work around the nose again until it is securely fixed.*

10 *Return to the instructions for the basic bear to work the mouth (steps 39–40). Using two strands of embroidery silk, take a $^3/_4$-in (2-cm) straight stitch downwards along the lower muzzle seam. Create a smiling mouth by taking two upward curving $^5/_8$-in (15-mm) stitches to left and right.*

11 *At basic bear steps 41 and 42, embroider the four claws on each paw and pad using six strands of terracotta embroidery thread. Each claw should be approximately 1 in (2.5 cm) long. Finally complete step 43, by lightly brushing your bear with a soft brush to remove any loose pile and re-check the clipping around the muzzle and eyes. If necessary clip again.*

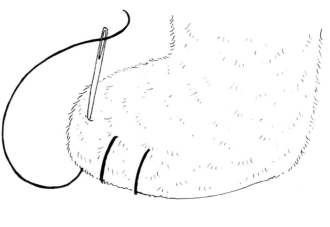

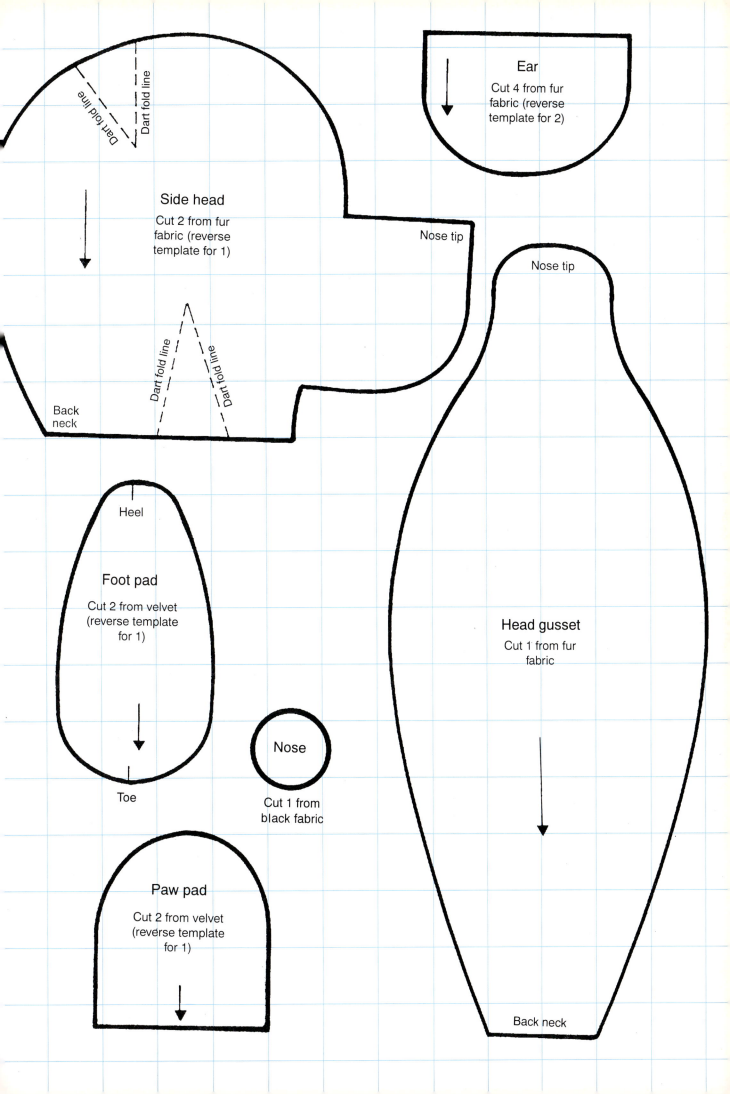

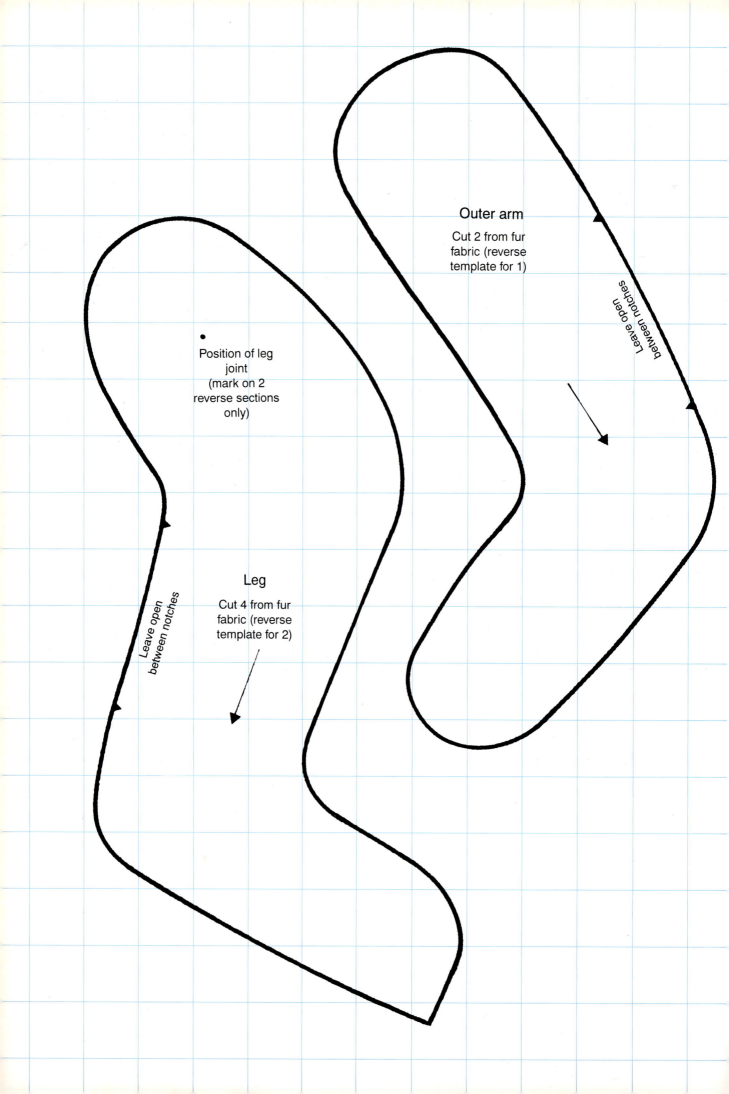

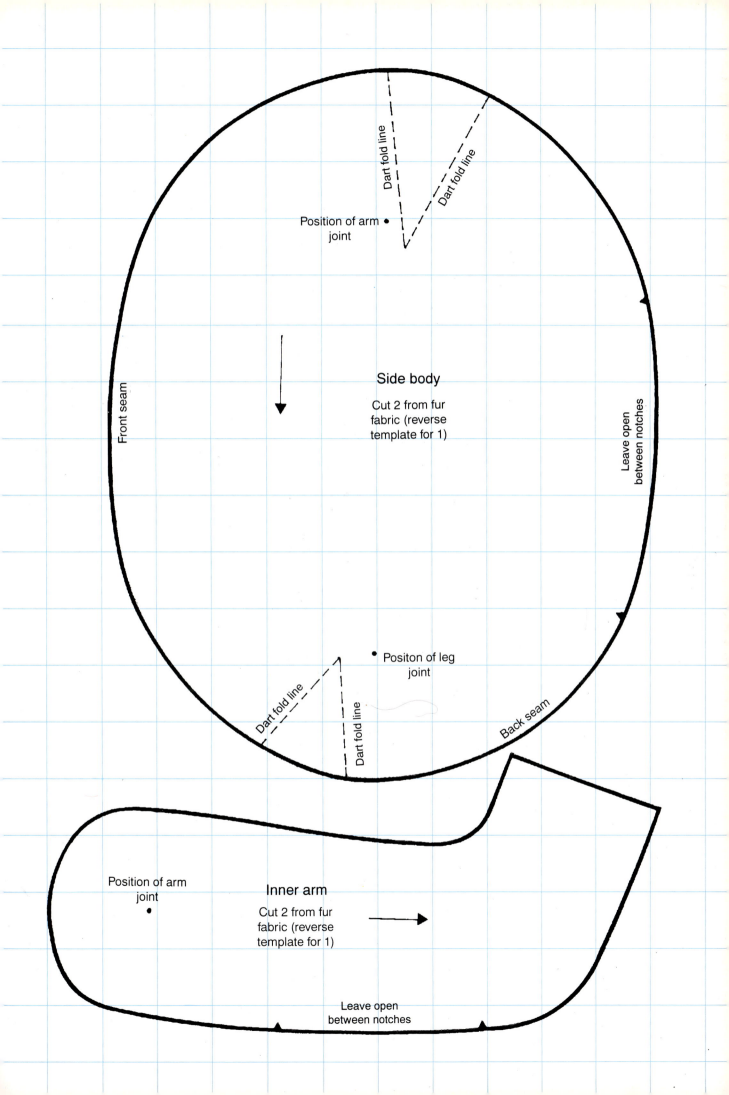

ROSE

Height 16 ½ in (42 cm)

This pinkish beige mohair bear, has paws and pads of fuschia-pink shot silk, shaded with apricot. Her muzzle is lightly trimmed to show her delightful heart-shaped nose and her bright chocolate-brown eyes. Rose is truly a boudoir bear, designed to sit prettily on a crisp cotton pillow, just waiting to be admired.

When making bears, it is pleasant to turn the attention to a specifically feminine character, designed to grace a teenage girl's bedroom. Such bears are particularly popular in America, where many bear-makers are producing pastel-coloured bears in luxury mohairs, silks and cashmeres.

The choice of fabric for a boudoir bear is critical. Wherever possible try to achieve a soft and delicate effect. Rich silks and satins are good choices for paws and pads. These colours and textures can be echoed in any accessories you select, making a pleasingly colour-coordinated bear. When working in pastel shades, be sure to take precautions to keep the fabric clean. Follow the advice given for Little Roger on page 58.

Feminine bears can be adorned with scraps of antique lace, strings of pearls and even feather boas. Scraps of antique textiles can often be found in the rummage boxes of antique shops and market stalls. These can be purchased relatively cheaply, and can greatly enhance your bear's appearance. Try not to overdo the effect, however. One small scrap of hand-made lace will have much more impact than yards of machine-made braid.

MATERIALS

In addition to the basic tools and materials listed on page 20,
you will also need the following:

½ yd (0.5 m) rose beige short-pile mohair
6-in (15-cm) square of fuschia shot silk
Tacking cotton to tone with fabric
All-purpose sewing thread to tone with fabric
Chalk pencil or tailor's chalk
One 60-mm hardboard joint

Two 40-mm hardboard joints
Two 50-mm hardboard joints
Strong polyester thread to tone with fabric
4 oz (100 g) polyester filling
1.1 lb (500 g) woodwool
Two light-brown glass eyes with black pupils
Fuschia silk embroidery thread

Enlarge the pattern pages by 40 per cent.

Clothed Bears

In the early 1900s the fashion designer Paul Poiret suggested that smart women should carry with them a beautifully costumed doll as a modish accessory. This novel idea was soon taken up by other couturiers and dolls were produced clothed in gowns by top designers. 'Boudoir Dolls' became the rage. The British toy firm of Dean's continued to make 'Smart set' dolls until 1928.

Bear manufacturers also followed this trend by clothing their bears. Their costumes, however, were more masculine, ranging from British sailors to Cossack soldiers. Clown and pierrot bears proved particularly popular. First described as 'a toy for boys', the teddy bear became the male counterpart to the little girl's doll. However, in a bid to attract a wider market, during the 1920s some manufacturers produced grotesque little creatures that were half doll and half bear. Failing to satisfy the market for either toy, their appeal was somewhat limited.

Special Instructions

1 Work to the basic bear instructions until step 11. Before placing the body sections together, pin the darts along the foldline. Tack and remove pins. Machine stitch along the dart foldline, using the reverse facility (if you have one) on your machine to start and finish. Press the darts towards the back of the body before joining the body sections as usual.

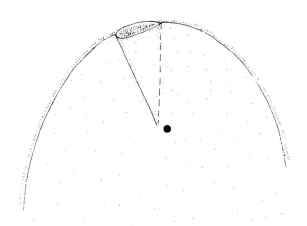

2 At basic bear step 27, use the 40-mm joints for the arms.

3 At basic bear step 31, place each eye just below the head gusset seam, approximately 1½ in (4 cm) from the nose tip. Trim the fur back around the eyes once they are secured.

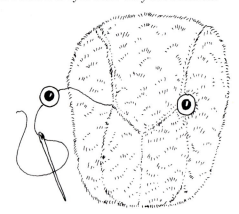

4 At basic bear step 34, set each ear with its inner edge on the head gusset seam about 4½ in (11.5 cm) from the nose tip.

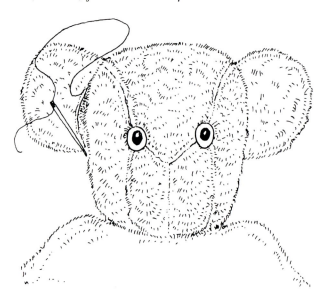

5 At basic bear step 36, trim only the fur on the nose tip to form a heart shape. The seamline around the head gusset will naturally form this shape. Work slowly and carefully, cutting just a few strands at a time until you are satisfied with the shape. The clipped area should measure approximately 1 in (2.5 cm) at its widest point and should extend about ¾ in (2 cm) down the front of the muzzle.

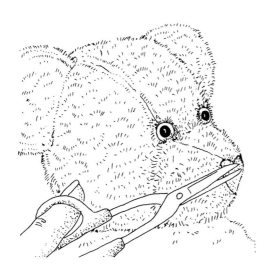

6 At basic bear steps 37 and 38, attach a single strand of embroidery thread and use the clipped shape as a guide. Work each side separately, using straight stitches to form a heart-shaped nose. Work over the area several times, until the shape is well padded. Take thread away from the nose tip and cut off in the normal way.

7 When working the mouth (basic bear, steps 39 and 40), use doubled thread. Take a straight stitch approximately ⅝ in (1.5 cm) in length downwards along the lower muzzle seamline. Form the mouth by taking a ⅜ in (1 cm) straight stitch to left and then to the right. Trim back the pile lightly around the muzzle tip to show the mouth stitching.

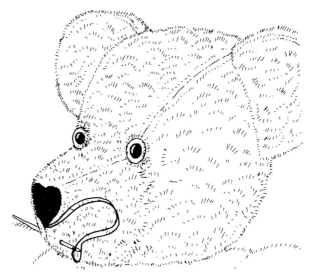

8 At basic bear steps 41 and 42, work the claws using the full thickness of the embroidery thread. The claws on the front paws should measure approximately ¾ in (2 cm). Those on the foot pads should measure 1 in (2.5-cm). Use a brush appropriate to the fabric to finish.

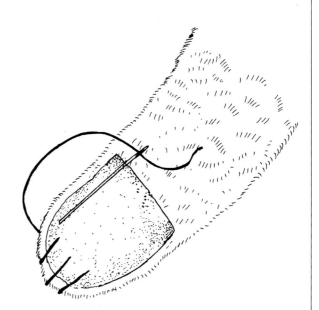

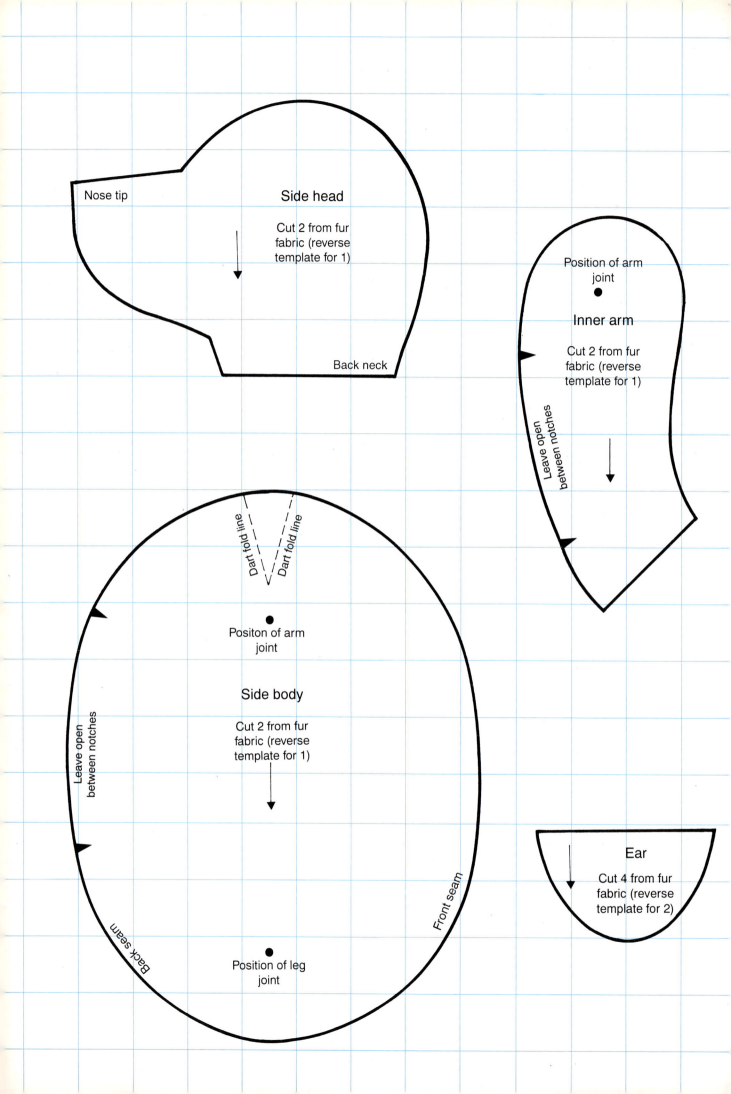

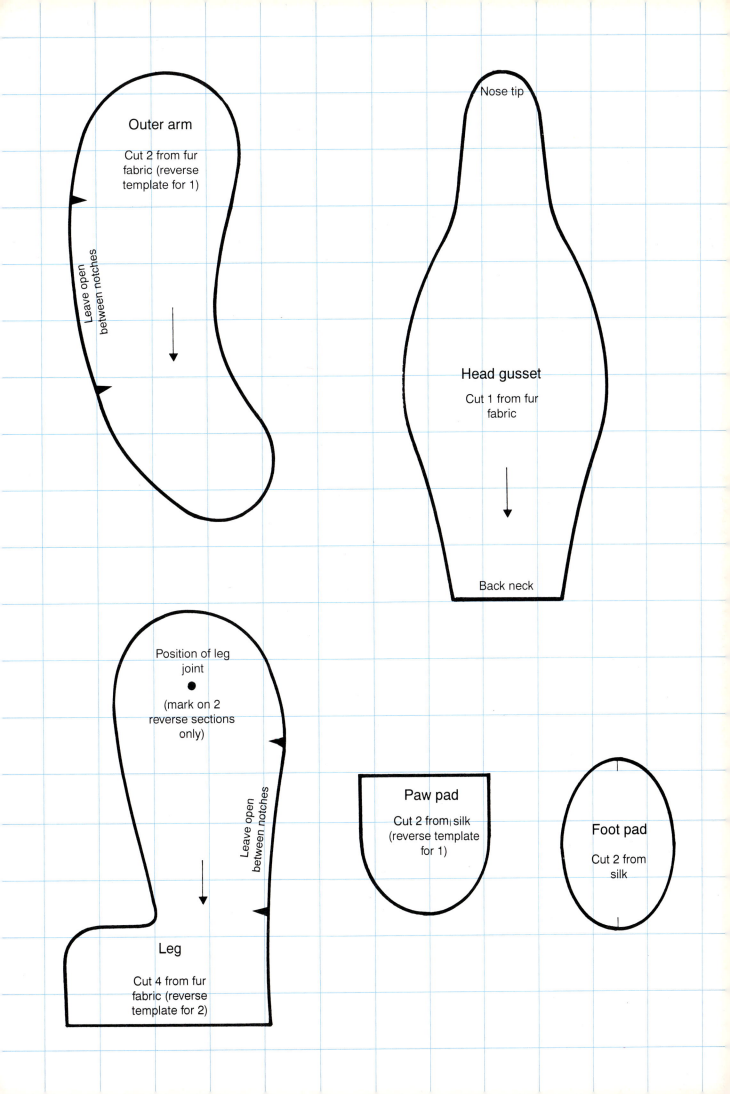

Theodore

Height 24 in (60 cm)

This bear was cut from a fake fur coat, recycled to make a delightful and endearing friend. A medium-length coat provides sufficient fabric to make one large and one small bear, or three to four medium-sized bears. Of course, any short length straight piled fabric can be used to produce the same effect, but because of his size you may prefer to use an inexpensive acrylic fabric, rather than a luxury mohair or silk mix.

You may find that some fake fur fabrics used for clothing have a very dense fur pile woven into a fairly stiff backing fabric. This can make tacking and machine stitching a little more difficult. Before stitching it is advisable to vacuum over both the right and wrong surfaces of the fabric, to remove any dust which may have accumulated, particularly if the coat has been hanging in a wardrobe for a long time. For strength use heavy-duty nylon thread for all seams.

The recycling of fabrics for toy-making is not a new idea. During World War II, when bears could no longer be imported from Europe, old garments were frequently used as materials for toy-making. So popular were home-made toys at this time, that many women's magazines published patterns for a wide range of items, such as rag dolls, elephants and, of course, teddy bears. One such post-war booklet, published while clothes rationing was still in force, recommended their readers to search their attics and trunks for discarded hats, old stockings and fur rugs. Times may not now be so hard, but there is immense satisfaction to be gained from making a thing of worth from an item of little intrinsic value. It may take a little extra time, but the results are very rewarding.

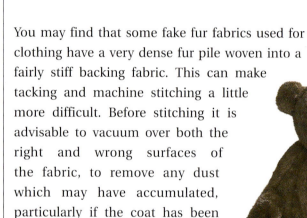

Materials

In addition to the basic tools and materials listed on page 20, you will also need the following:

1 yd (1 m) 5-mm straight-pile acrylic or mohair in dark brown
Tacking cotton to tone with fabric
9-inch (23-cm) square of black velvet
All-purpose black sewing thread
Five 64-mm hardboard joints

Heavy-duty brown nylon thread
8 oz (250 g) polyester filling
8 oz (250 g) woodwool
8 oz (250 g) plastic pellets
Two 18-mm black glass boot-button eyes
Black perle embroidery thread

Enlarge the pattern pages by 40 per cent.

DARK BEARS

The original 'bruins' of the 19th century were made from dark brown or black fur, some indeed used real bear skins. Since these early days, most manufacturers have included a dark-furred bear in their range at some time.

Many of the black and dark brown bears of the early 1900s featured black, boot-button eyes set on circles of orange or red felt. These early bears were reminiscent of the clockwork automata made in France and Germany. The bright colouring of the felt was intended to make the eyes more prominent, but often resulted in a somewhat ferocious expression.

SPECIAL INSTRUCTIONS

1 Work to step 4 of the instructions for the basic bear. If using an old fake fur coat to make this bear, unpick and discard the lining fabric before drawing out the pattern pieces. Remove the arms and collar and unpick all side seams. Lay the fabric flat and proceed as usual. Make sure that the pile lies straight on the upper arm pieces. The nose, paws and pads are cut from black velvet. The pile should run from toe to heel on the pads and from finger tips to wrist on the paws.

2 At basic bear step 11, before placing the side head sections together, pin the darts along the foldline. Tack and remove pins. Stitch along the dart foldline, using your machine's reverse facility, if available, to start and finish. Press the darts towards the back of the head before joining the two side head sections.

3 At basic bear step 13, before placing the side body sections together, pin the darts along the foldline. Tack and stitch as for the head darts. Press the darts towards the back of the body before joining the two body sections.

4 When stitching the pads and paws (basic bear, steps 15 and 16), wherever possible machine stitch with the fur fabric against the feed dogs, as these can snag delicate fabrics such as velvet. If in any doubt, hand sew pads and paws, using a heavy-duty thread and small back stitches.

5 At basic bear step 19, the exaggerated shape of the arms may make turning difficult and great care must be taken not to pierce the velvet with the turning tools. Turn the top section first and then gently ease the paw section inwards and upwards through the stuffing hole. Once this is through, the rest of the arm should follow more easily. Use your fingers wherever possible to tease the bunched fabric through a little at a time. Continue with the basic instructions until you are ready to stuff the limbs.

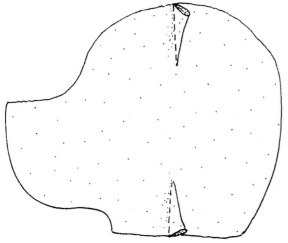
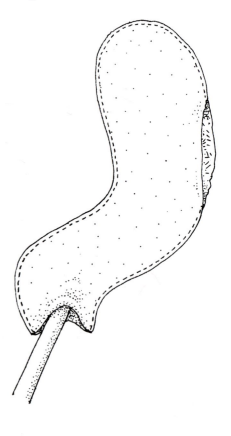

6 Omit basic bear steps 27 and 28 and follow the special instructions 2, 3 and 4 given for Bertie on page 66 for stuffing with polyester filling and pellets. Ladder stitch the limbs closed.

8 At basic bear step 34, place each ear across the head gusset seam just in front of the shaping darts, about 3 1/2 in (9 cm) from the centre of each eye. One third of the ear width should lie on the head gusset. After stitching the back seam of each ear to the head, insert a small amount of polyester filling. Turn in the front seam allowance and stitch securely into position (basic bear, step 35).

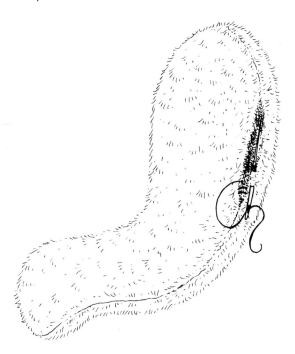

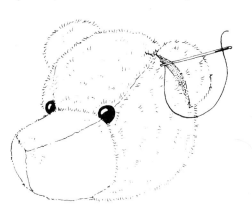

9 Omit basic bear steps 37 and 38. Cut the nose from a 2-in (5-cm) circle of velvet. Stuff and gather as described for Bertie, Special instructions 9 and 10 (page 68). Slip stitch into position across the nose tip seam, using doubled heavy-duty thread. Pull tightly and fasten off securely.

7 At basic bear step 31, place each eye across the head gusset seam, just as it widens to form the forehead, about 2 in (5 cm) from the nose tip. Attach the eyes in the usual way.

10 Return to the basic bear instructions to work the mouth (step 39). Use a doubled length of perle embroidery thread. Take a 1 3/8-in (3.5-cm) straight stitch downwards along the lower muzzle seam. Take the needle back up to the starting point and make a second stitch, so that four threads lie side by side to give extra definition. Take a 3/4-in (2-cm) straight stitch to either side to form a T-shaped mouth. As this bear has no claws, omit basic bear steps 41 and 42.

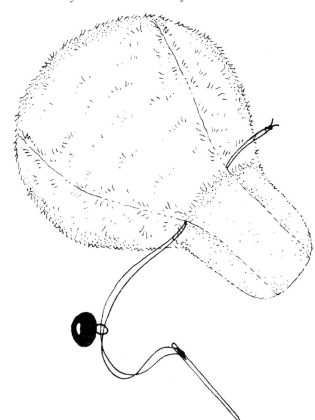

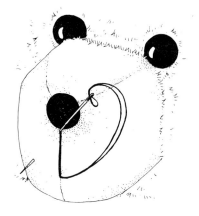

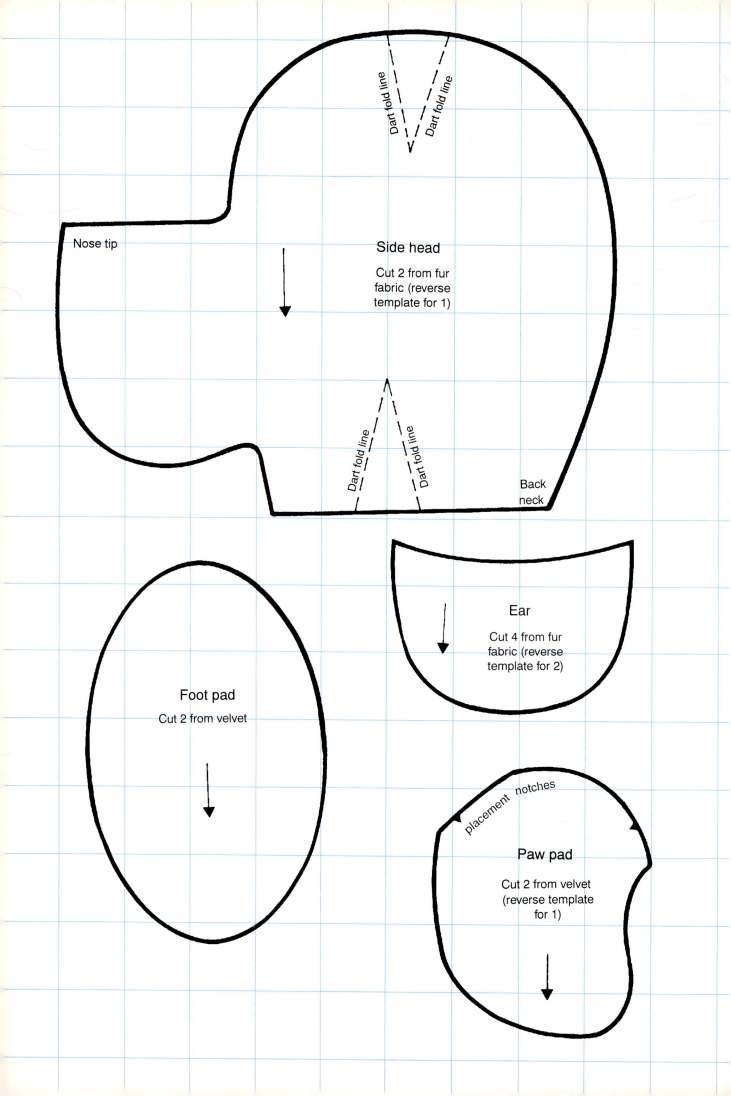

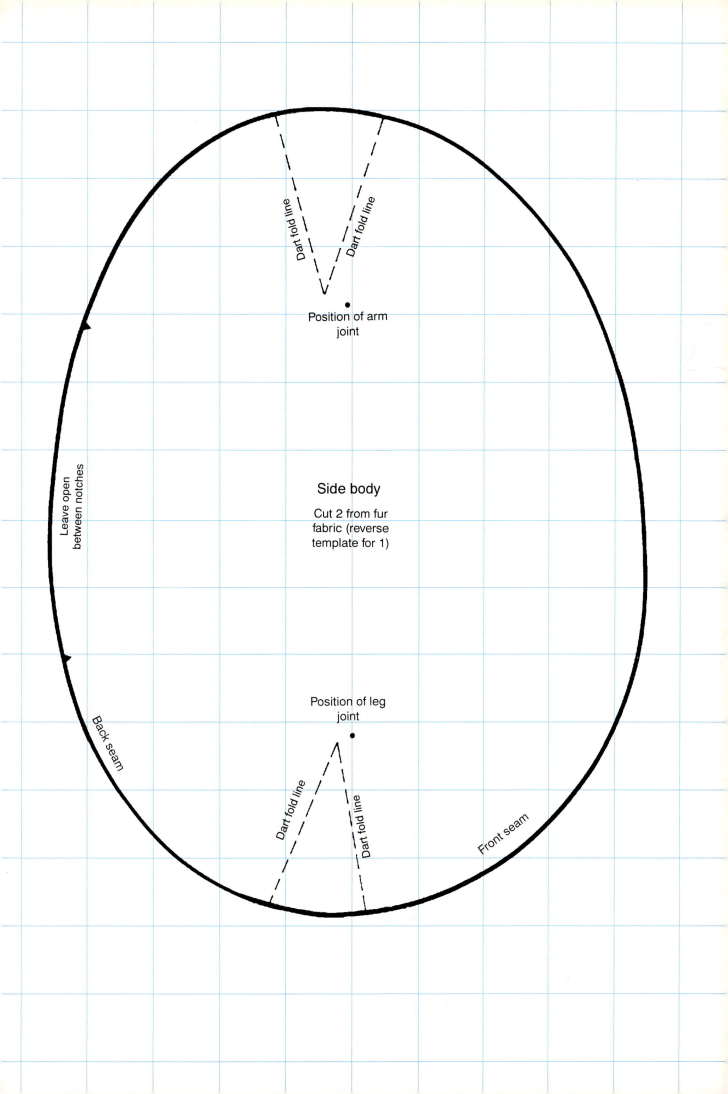

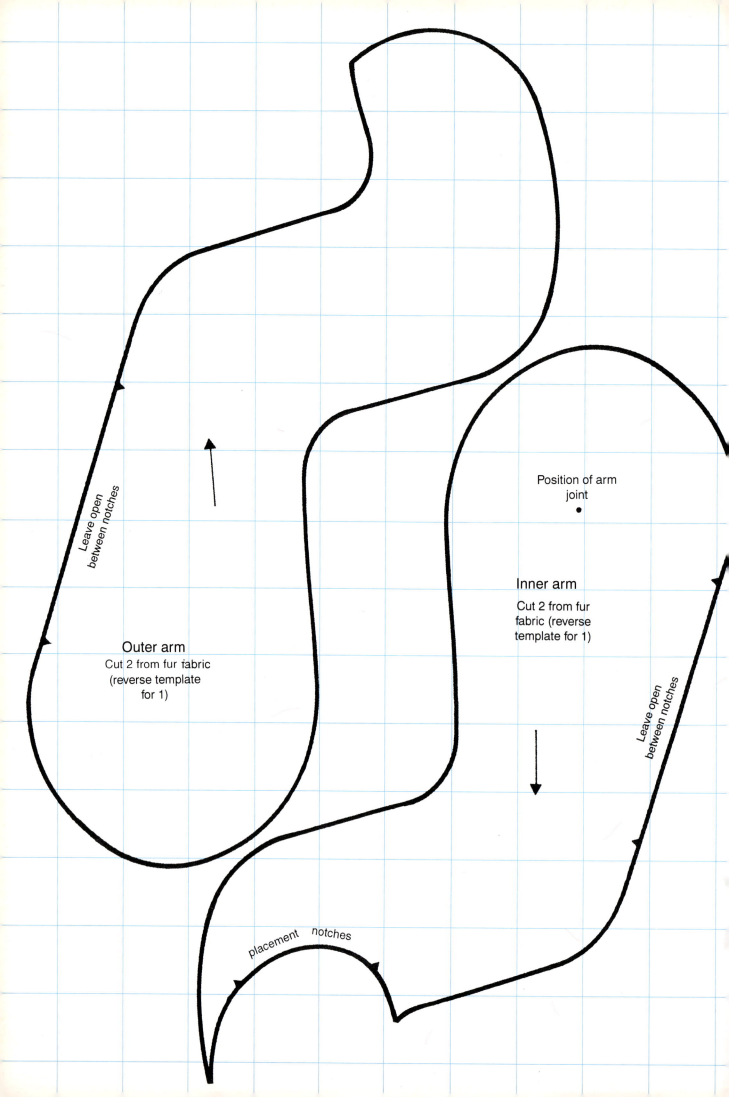

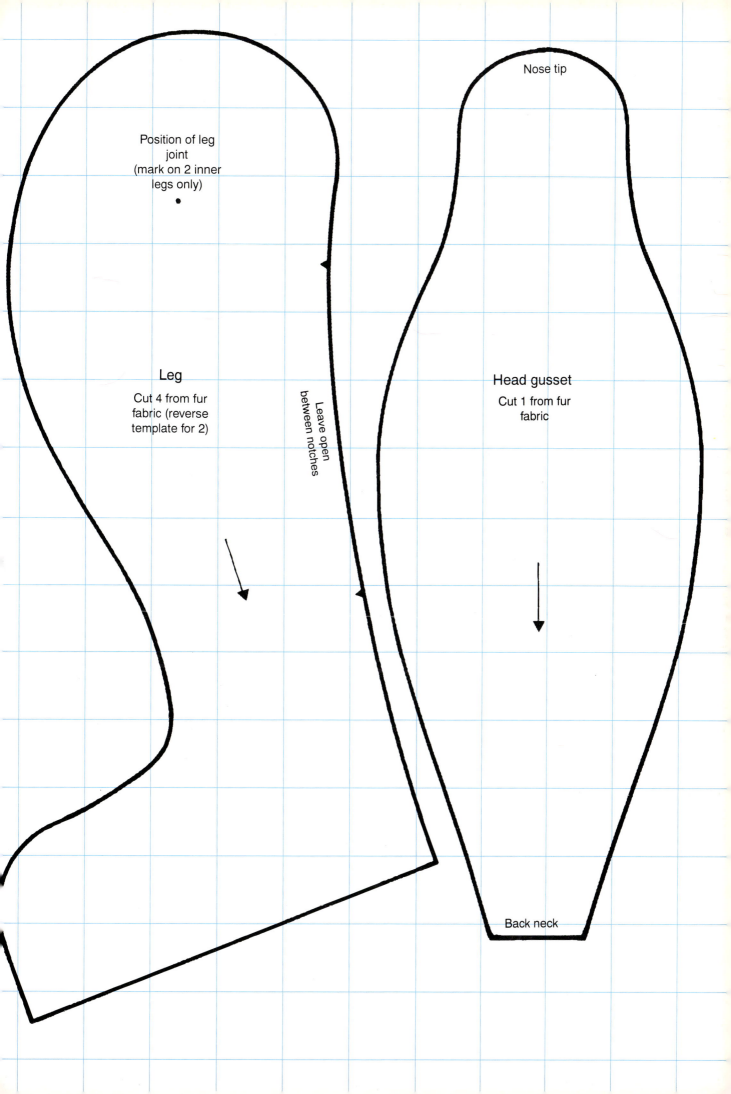

EDWARD
Height 21 in (52 cm)

Fitted with a Swiss movement musical box that plays 'Teddy Bear's Picnic', Edward is a prince among bears. His superb dark-brown mohair coat is complemented by large pads and paws of coffee-coloured German felt. His long, thin legs and unusually shaped arms are filled with a mixture of polyester and pellets, but his firm body is tightly stuffed with woodwool.

Musical boxes can be fitted to any bear with a large enough body. In order to hold the mechanism securely, the body must be stuffed with woodwool. When in position, the musical box should fit tightly against the back of the bear, so that the winding key protrudes free of the fur fabric surface. This is particularly important when making a bear from long-pile fabric. It is also essential that the box is well padded to prevent friction during use that could damage the fabric.

MATERIALS

In addition to the basic tools and materials listed on page 20, you will also need the following:

½ yd (0.5 m) dark-brown short-pile mohair
Tacking cotton to tone with fabric
All-purpose sewing thread to tone with fabric
Three 65-mm hardboard joints
Two 80-mm hardboard joints
Strong polyester thread to tone with fabric
8-in (20-cm) square of coffee-coloured felt
8 oz (250 g) polyester filling

2 lb (1 kg) woodwool
8 oz (250 g) plastic pellets
Two 18-mm black boot button eyes
Heavy-duty nylon thread
Black perle embroidery thread
Fine silk embroidery thread
6-in (15-cm) square of muslin
Small square musical movement with wind-up key

Enlarge the pattern pages by 40 per cent.

Musical Bears

The first musical bears appeared before the 1930s. They were fitted with mechanisms that were wound up by a protruding key, which turned an internal cylinder against a set of metal teeth to produce a tune. The more complicated the tune, the more notes or teeth were required. Most modern movements produce tunes containing 12 to 18 notes. Old musical boxes were fitted inside boxes made of wood and metal, but today's covers are more usually of plastic, although the movements are usually still driven by traditional Swiss clockwork mechanisms.

Many other forms of clockwork mechanism have been used in toy bears. Automata, tumbling and walking bears, together with novelties such as the Schuco Skating bear, command high prices at auction, particularly if they are still in fine working condition. It is said that these skating bears, also made by the Bing factory, were inspired by a real bear called Alice, who was famous for performing on roller skates in the United States during the early 20th century.

Special Instructions

1 Follow the instructions for the basic bear until step 10. Before placing the side head sections together, pin the darts along the foldline. Tack and remove pins. Stitch along the dart foldline, using your machine's reverse facility, if available, to start and finish. Press the darts towards the back of the head before joining the two side head sections.

2 At basic bear step 11, before placing the side body sections together, pin the darts along the foldline. Tack and stitch as for the head darts. Press the darts towards the back of the body before joining the two body sections.

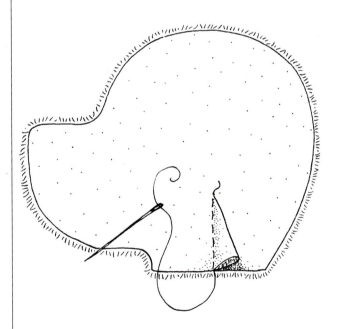

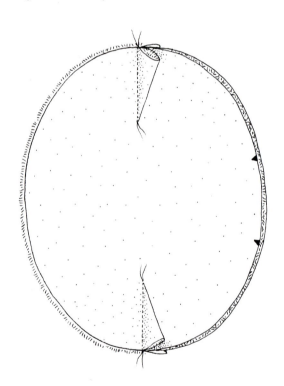

3 At basic bear step 18, the unusual shape of the arms, may mean that turning is more difficult than usual. Use a blunt-ended stuffing stick to ease the fabrics through gently, being careful not to damage the more delicate felt of the paws. Do not use too much force. Continue with the instructions for the basic bear.

4 At basic bear step 27, the hardboard discs of the arm joints need to be positioned carefully because they are large. If you have trouble inserting the assembled section of the joint, push the disc into position first and then carefully insert the split pin and washer. Then push the tip of the split pin through the hole already made in the ground fabric.

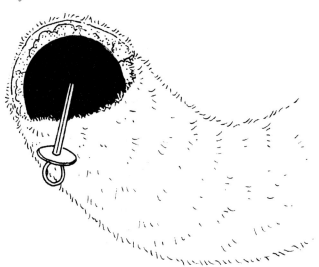

5 Pack the head of the joint with polyester filling (basic bear, step 28) in place of woodwool. Then follow the special instructions 2, 3 and 4 given for Bertie on page 66 for stuffing the limbs with pellets. Return to basic instructions.

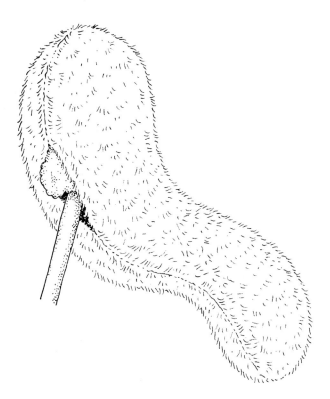

6 At basic bear step 30, begin stuffing the body firmly with woodwool. Use a stuffing stick to pack the filling down as hard as you can. Once you reach the lower edge of the stuffing opening, start to push woodwool into the front of the body, forming a cavity into which the musical box can be placed.

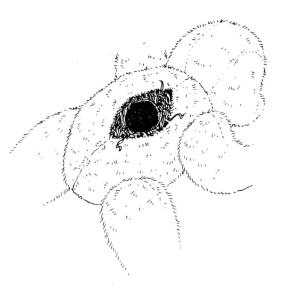

7 Cut a circle of muslin large enough to enclose the musical box and run a line of small tacking stitches around the edge. Do not fasten off. Place the musical box in the centre of the piece of muslin and draw the thread up a little to form a small pouch. Pack the pouch lightly with teased out polyester filling. Be sure to cover any sharp edges and corners.

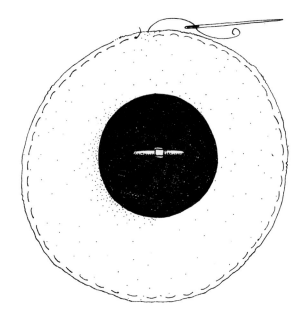

8 Once the pouch is filled, draw up the edges of the muslin around the protruding musical box key. Make a few straight stitches back and forth across the opening to secure and fasten off with several oversewing stitches.

10 At basic bear step 30, ladder stitch the stuffing opening closed a little at a time, continuing to add stuffing material where necessary. A few small balls of polyester filling can be added to fill any last minute depressions or gaps that may form as the back seam is finished.

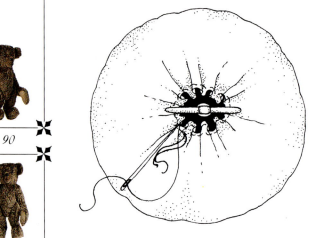

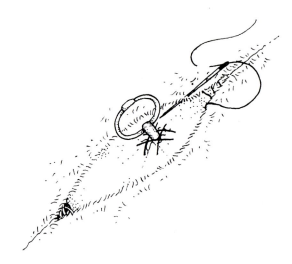

9 Place the musical box into the body cavity so that the key protrudes from the stuffing opening and the musical box rests against the back body fabric. Continue stuffing the body in the usual way, being careful to pack firmly around the musical box to prevent it from slipping.

11 At basic bear step 31, place each eye on the head gusset seam 1³⁄₄ in (4.5 cm) from the nose tip, so that their lower edge touches the point where the trimmed area of the muzzle begins. Attach the eyes as usual, and trim back the fur pile a little if necessary.

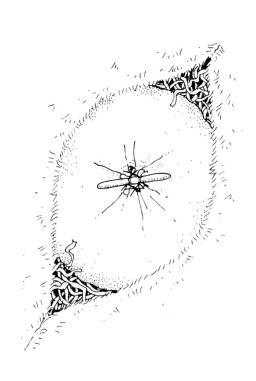

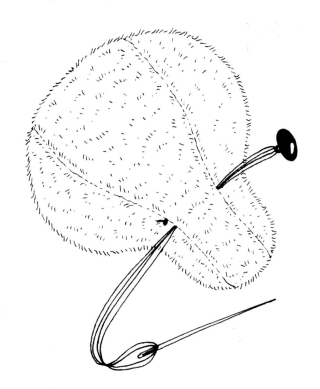

12 At basic bear step 34, place the ears so that the inner edge touches the head gusset seam and the outer edge is level with the nose, about 4½ in (11.5 cm) from the muzzle tip.

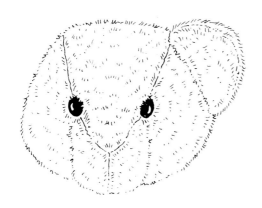

13 Trim back the muzzle (basic bear, step 36) to reveal the ground fabric to a depth of 1⅛ in (3 cm) across the upper nose tip and to a depth of 2⅜ in (6 cm) on each side of the muzzle.

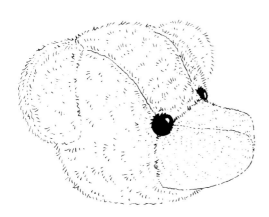

14 At basic bear step 37, embroider the nose under the nose tip seam using a single strand of perle embroidery thread. Work straight stitches over the area several times to produce a rectangle measuring 1⅛ in (3 cm) across and ¾ in (2 cm) down.

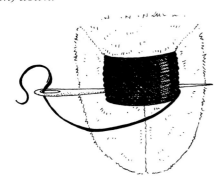

15 Form the mouth (basic bear, step 39) using two strands of perle embroidery thread. Take a single straight stitch, ¾ in (2 cm) long, downwards along the lower muzzle seam. Work a slightly curved long stitch, ¾ in (2 cm) long, upwards to either side, to form a smile.

16 Embroider claws on each paw and pad (basic bear, steps 41 and 42) using fine silk embroidery thread. The claws on the pads should measure about 1¼ in (3.5 cm) and those on the paws about ¾ in (2 cm). On large pads it looks more effective to graduate the length of the claws around the foot. Complete your bear by brushing (basic bear, step 43).

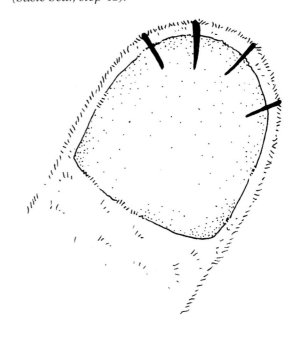

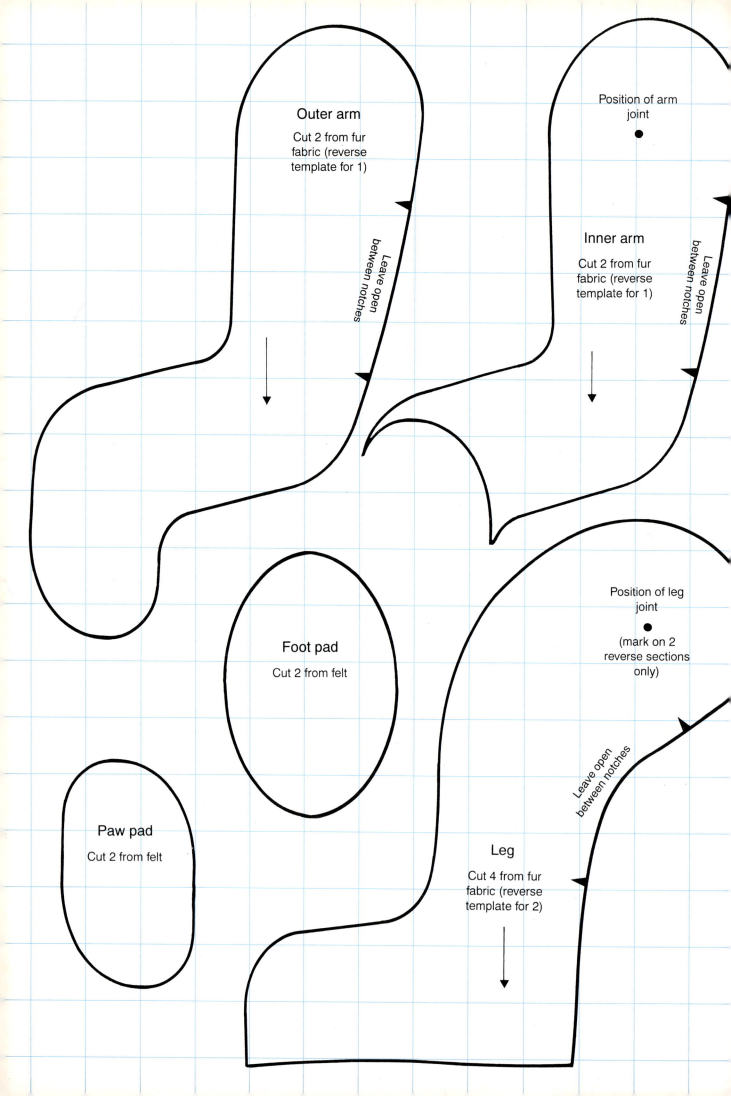

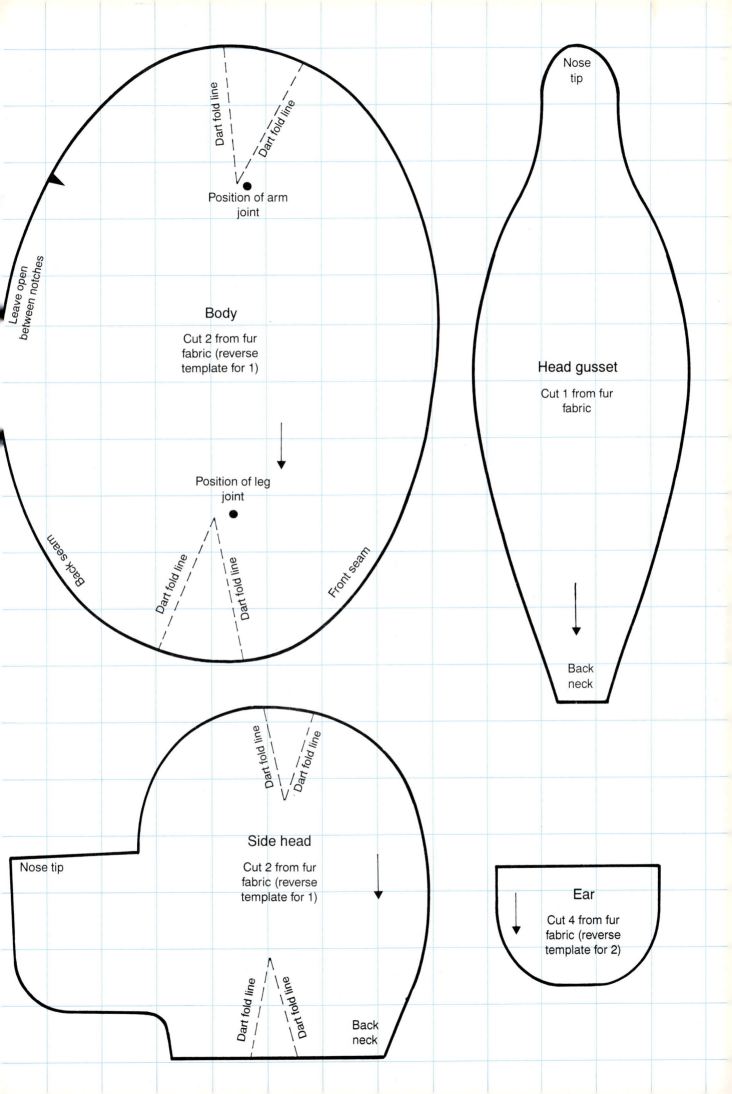

OSCAR

Height 20 in (50 cm)

O scar is a big brave bear, who growls when tipped backwards. Fitting a growler is a simple step that is performed just before the centre back seam is closed. This bear's wide, round body is perfect for adding a 'voice' mechanism. Plenty of woodwool needs to be packed around the growler to prevent it from slipping out of position with repeated use.

Always try out a growler before you buy. They can be purchased in three sizes – small, medium and large, depending on the size of your bear. Most sound more like the bleat of a goat or the moo of a cow than the growl of a bear, but some are more realistic than others. Most old growlers sound little more life-like than the modern versions, so you can be reassured that your bear's voice, if not authentic, is at least traditional.

In addition to the traditional growler, there are several types of plastic squeakers available for smaller bears. These are not really suitable for inclusion in an heirloom bear, but they can be used successfully in soft, polyester bears made as children's toys. Squeakers operate on the same basic principle of air forced through a reed, but are operated by pressure on the bear's tummy.

MATERIALS

In addition to the basic tools and materials listed on page 20,
you will also need the following:

½ yd (0.5 m) 'old gold' antique-pile mohair
9-in (25-cm) square of pale brown felt
All-purpose sewing thread to tone with fabric
One 80-mm hardboard joint
Two 65-mm hardboard joints
Two 70-mm hardboard joints
Strong polyester thread to tone with fabric

8 oz (250 g) polyester filling
2 lb (1 kg) woodwool
Two 16-mm black glass boot-button eyes
Medium-weight black embroidery thread
6-in (15-cm) square of muslin or calico
One large growler

Enlarge the pattern pages by 40 per cent.

Growling Bears

Early growlers consisted of a simple oilcloth bag that acted as a bellows, forcing air through a reed when the bear was punched. However, today's bears fitted with modern growlers will growl obediently when tipped backwards and forwards.

The German company, Bing, was one of the first to include a voice box in their bears, producing a dark brown mohair plush bear fitted with a tilt growler in 1911. Growlers at this time were made of cardboard with a circular speaker hole at one end of the cylinder, over which was glued a small piece of loosely woven gauze. Growlers have changed very little since their introduction and despite the fact that they emit a sound that is unlike that of any bear, they have remained a popular method of giving bears a voice.

Special Instructions

1 At basic bear step 5, pay careful attention to the placing of the templates on your fabric, as this bear will require the full amount of material. There is no allowance for error as there would be with a smaller bear. Pay particular attention to the placing of the arms, which are angled to indicate a wrist. When placing the arm templates, try to ensure that the pile runs straight down the upper arm. Once you are happy with the layout, continue to follow the basic bear instructions until step 11.

2 At basic bear step 10, place the two back body pieces right sides together and pin, leaving the seam open between the notches. Tack and remove pins. Place the two front body sections right sides together and pin. Tack and remove pins. Machine stitch both pairs of pieces before joining front and back sections as for the basic bear.

3 At basic bear step 30, pack the filling into the body until you reach the back opening. Continue stuffing the front section of the body to the arm joints, pushing the woodwool well forwards.

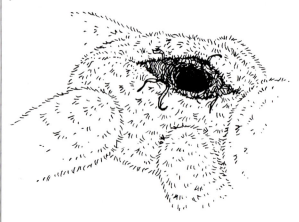

4 Cut the muslin or calico into a rough circle, large enough to enclose the growler. Run a line of tacking stitches around the edge of the circle, leaving the needle and thread attached.

5 Place the growler, perforated end downwards, in the centre of the circle of muslin or calico. Lightly cover with a little polyester filling and draw the threads up to form a bag. Fasten off securely and cut the thread.

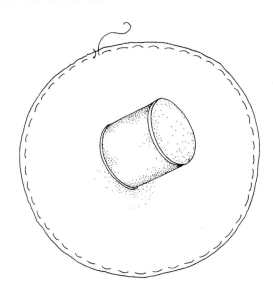

6 Insert the growler into the body cavity, so that the perforated top faces outwards, pushing it well down into the woodwool filling. Before completing the stuffing, fix the calico cover in place with a few tiny oversewing stitches into the ground fabric from inside the bear. Finish stuffing the body and close the back opening with ladder stitches in the normal manner. Add a little extra polyester filling as you work, to prevent the growler from rubbing against the fabric.

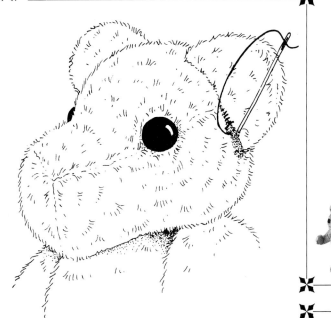

7 At basic bear step 31, set the eyes just above the head gusset seam, approximately 2³⁄₄ in (7 cm) from the nose tip.

9 At basic bear, step 37, use a doubled length of medium embroidery thread to work a large rectangle, measuring 1 ¹⁄₈ in across by 1 in deep (3 cm x 2.5 cm) to form the nose. Start at the front curve of the head gusset and work downwards across the lower muzzle seam. Work over this rectangle several times to make the nose look slightly padded.

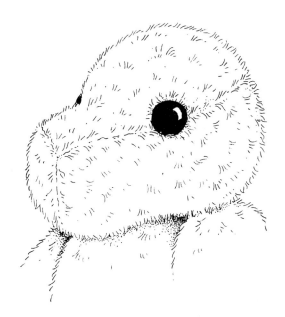

8 Position the ears (basic bear, step 37) so that the inner two thirds of each ear lies across the head gusset, approximately 5 ¹⁄₂ in (14 cm) from the muzzle tip.

10 Using two strands of thread, take a 1-in (2.5-cm) straight stitch downwards along the lower muzzle seam and form the mouth by making a T shape with straight stitches to either side (basic bear, steps 39 and 40). These stitches should each measure 1 in (2.5 cm) and be left slack to create a smile. Omit basic bear steps 41 and 43, as this bear has no claws. Finish by brushing (basic bear, step 43).

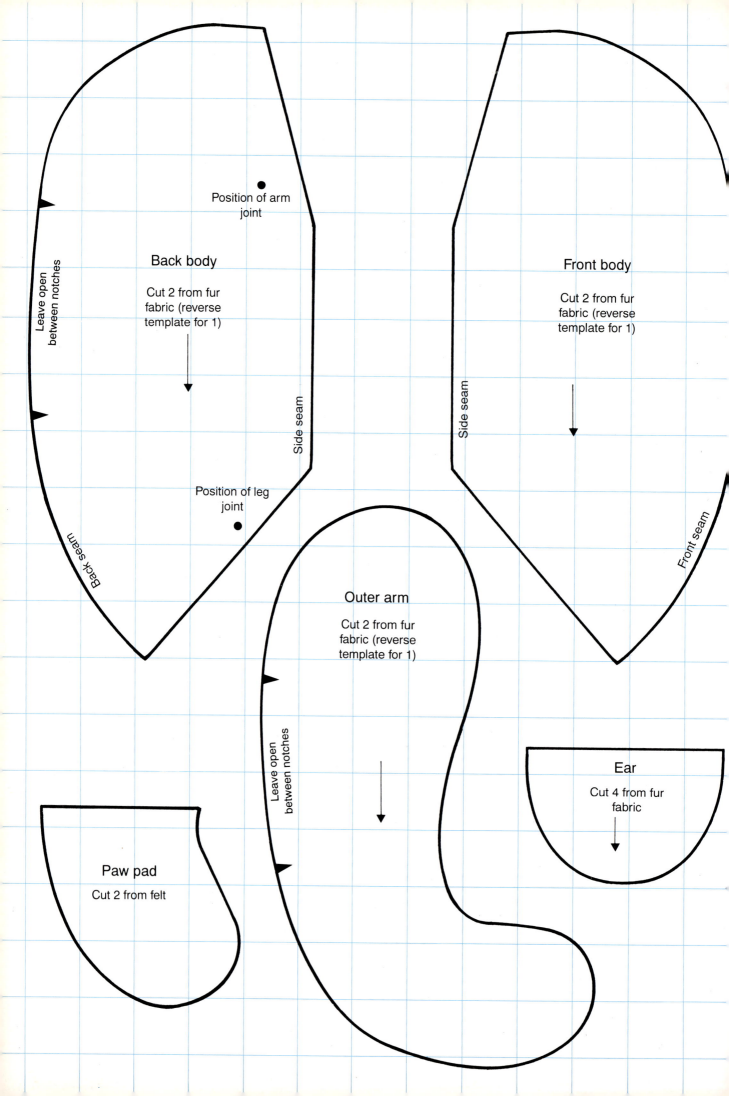

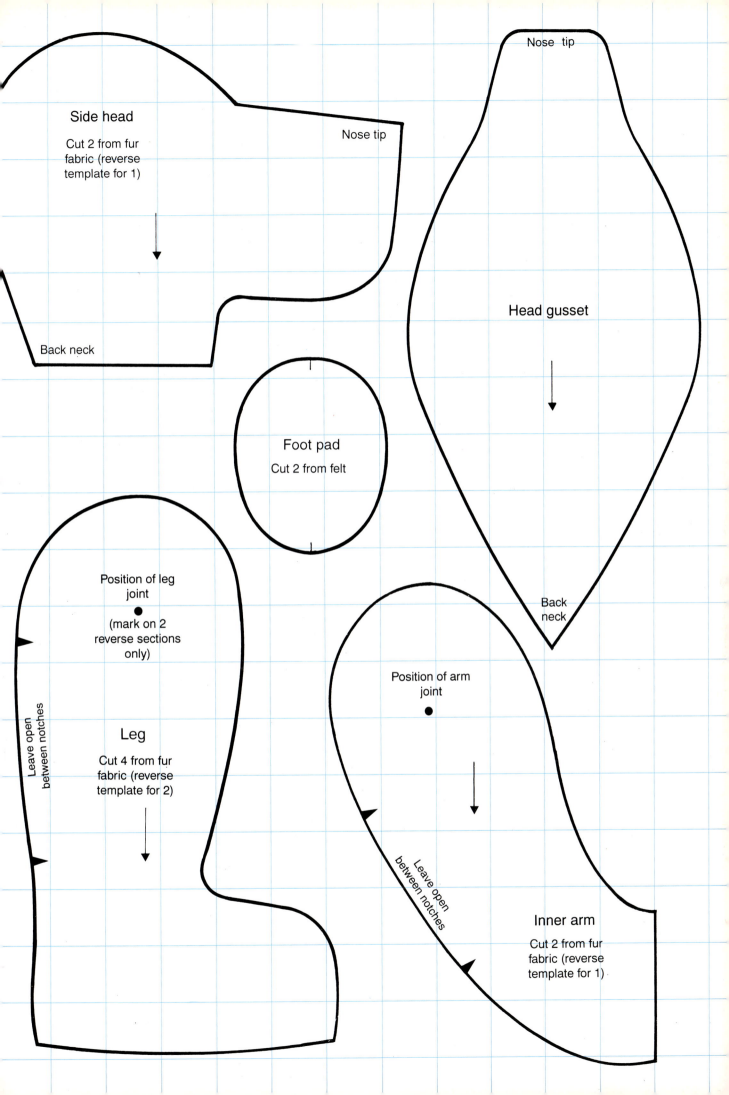

SAMUEL

Height 20 in (50 cm)

This delightful bear is made from dense, long-pile mohair in a faded gold colour. Samuel is designed as a child's bear. He has safety locking joints and eyes, which comply with modern safety requirements. He is stuffed with a hygienic, flame-retardant, polyester filling, and is soft and comforting to hold. Samuel can also be made as a collector's bear, by substituting hardboard joints, glass eyes and woodwool stuffing. Do remember, however, that the bear will then no longer be a suitable plaything for children under the age of ten years.

This bear has been made according to the instructions for the basic bear on pages 20-33, with the exception of those relating to fitting the eyes and joints. The special instructions given in this section refer to the use of materials that comply with current European safety regulations governing the production of children's toys. Although the instructions here refer to *Samuel*, the same toy-safe techniques can be applied to any bear in this book.

Mohair fabric should not be washed. If you want to make a washable bear, substitute a high-quality acrylic fabric for the mohair and a fast-dyed cotton or polyester material for the pads and paws. Most pure silks are not colour fast, so always use a deep-dyed cotton or linen thread to embroider the features of a bear that is intended to be washable. The use of plastic joints and eyes will ensure that the completed bear can be machine-washed and gently tumble-dried.

MATERIALS

In addition to the basic tools and materials listed on page 20,
you will also need the following:

³⁄₄ yd (0.75 m) 'faded gold' 1-in (25-mm) pile mohair
9-in (25-cm) square of pale cream felt
Two ³⁄₄-in (18-mm) black buttons
Two 18-mm plastic safety eyes
Safety-eye tool OR cotton reel
Tacking cotton to tone with fabric
All-purpose sewing thread to tone with fabric

One 65-mm plastic safety-locking joint
Four 50-mm plastic safety-locking joints
Safety-joint tool OR large empty wooden cotton reel
Strong polyester thread to tone with fabric
2 lb (1 kg) flame-retardant polyester filling
Matt-black cotton embroidery thread

Enlarge the pattern pages by 40 per cent.

Toy-Safe Bears

Until the end of World War II, children had taken their chances with what, by today's standards, would seem to be fairly hazardous toys. In the late 1940s, the British firm, Wendy Boston Playsafe Toy Co., which had developed the first metal-locking eye mechanism, became the first company to patent a child-safe plastic eye. After this time, all toys were subject to new health, safety and hygiene regulations.

Many fabric manufacturers were also struggling to improve the quality of the synthetic fabrics used for bears. In order to meet these requirements, another British Company, Dean's Childsplay, produced a high-quality Bri-nylon bear, while in the United States the massive Monsanto Company developed their own fabric, Acrilan. These man-made, washable fabrics were seen as a great step forward. Leading the field, once more, the Wendy Boston Toy Company, using nylon fabric and latex foam filling, made a further break-through by producing the first completely machine-washable bear. Taking full advantage of the advertising potential of her products to the house-proud mothers of the 1950s, Wendy Boston's bears flourished.

2. Before stuffing the bear (basic bear, step 20), insert the safety eyes. Stuff the muzzle with a small amount of polyester filling to the point at which the face broadens and flattens. This will be approximately 2 in (5 cm) from the nose tip. Mark each eye placement point on the outer edge of each head gusset side seam with a black button. Secure these with a glass-headed pin until satisfied with the effect. Remove the button, leaving the glass-headed pin as a marker. Ease the threads apart with a stiletto or knitting needle and cut only enough threads to allow the tight passage of the eye shank. Remove the glass-headed pin. It may be necessary to cut a few threads of the ground fabric to accommodate the shank of the eye. Push the eye shank through the fabric. Remove the polyester filling from the muzzle, turn the head inside out and secure the eye by threading on the locking washer over the shank tip, with its triangular segments pointing upwards. Use a safety-eye tool or a cotton reel to push the washer down firmly. Check the position of the second eye carefully and secure it in the same manner.

Special Instructions

1. At basic bear step 11, before placing the side body sections together, pin the darts along the foldline. Tack and stitch using the reverse facility on your machine (if available) to start and finish. Press the darts towards the back of the body before joining the two body sections.

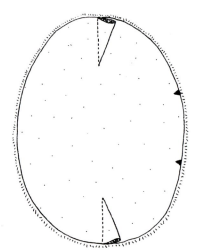

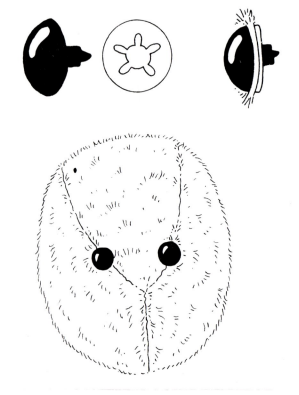

3 *Continue to follow the basic instructions for stuffing the bear and inserting the joints (basic bear, steps 20 to 26), substituting the safety-locking joints for hardboard joints where required. To use a safety-locking joint for the neck, follow the same instructions for securing the first half of the joint as if it were a hardboard joint (basic bear, steps 23 and 24), running a draw thread around the base of the neck. Pull the thread up tightly and finish by taking large straight stitches back and forth across the joint opening. To accommodate the thicker shank of the safety-locking joint, a larger hole than usual is needed, either in the intersection of the body seams or in the body fabric at the placement point. Take care to cut only a few threads at a time. Push the shank through the hole, thread on the large plastic disc and, using a safety tool or cotton reel, complete the joint by pushing the locking washer down very tightly. Always be sure to position each plastic joint correctly before threading on the locking washer. Once assembled they are almost impossible to undo.*

5 *Since the eyes are already in place, omit basic bear steps 31 to 33. At step 34, the inner third of each ear should be placed across the head gusset, with the remaining two thirds running vertically downwards along the side of the head. Place the inner edge of each about 4 in (10 cm) from each eye. Attach the ears in the usual way.*

6 *Clip the muzzle in an oval (basic bear, step 36) and embroider the nose using six strands of embroidery thread to form a vertical rectangle measuring ⅝ in by ¾ in (15 mm x 20 mm).*

7 *At basic bear steps 39 and 40, form the mouth with a ⅝-in (15-mm) straight stitch downwards along the lower muzzle seam. Take a ¾-in (20-mm) straight stitch upwards and outwards to the right and left. Omit steps 41 and 42, and finish by brushing (basic bear, step 43).*

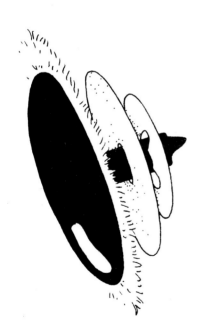

4 *Assemble the joints for all limbs in the same way (basic bear, steps 27–29), using the positioning points marked on the pattern pieces for inner arm, inner legs and body. Before stuffing the body, check that all the locking washers are as tightly positioned as possible. Stuff the body with polyester filling (basic bear, step 30).*

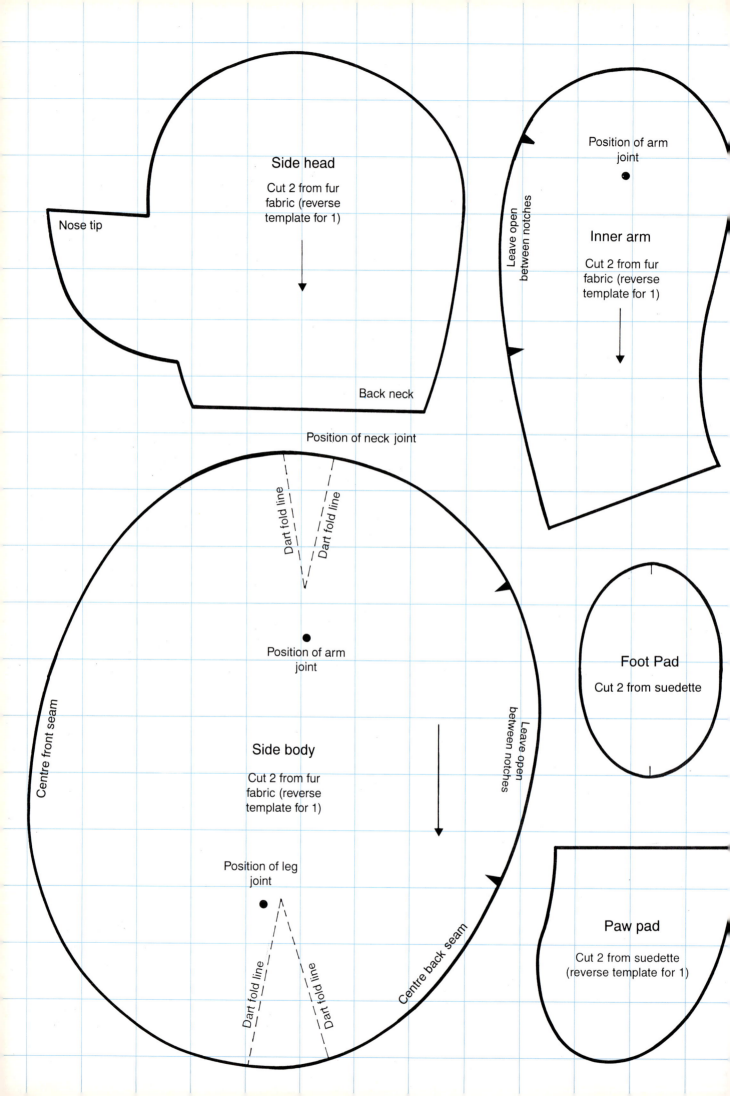

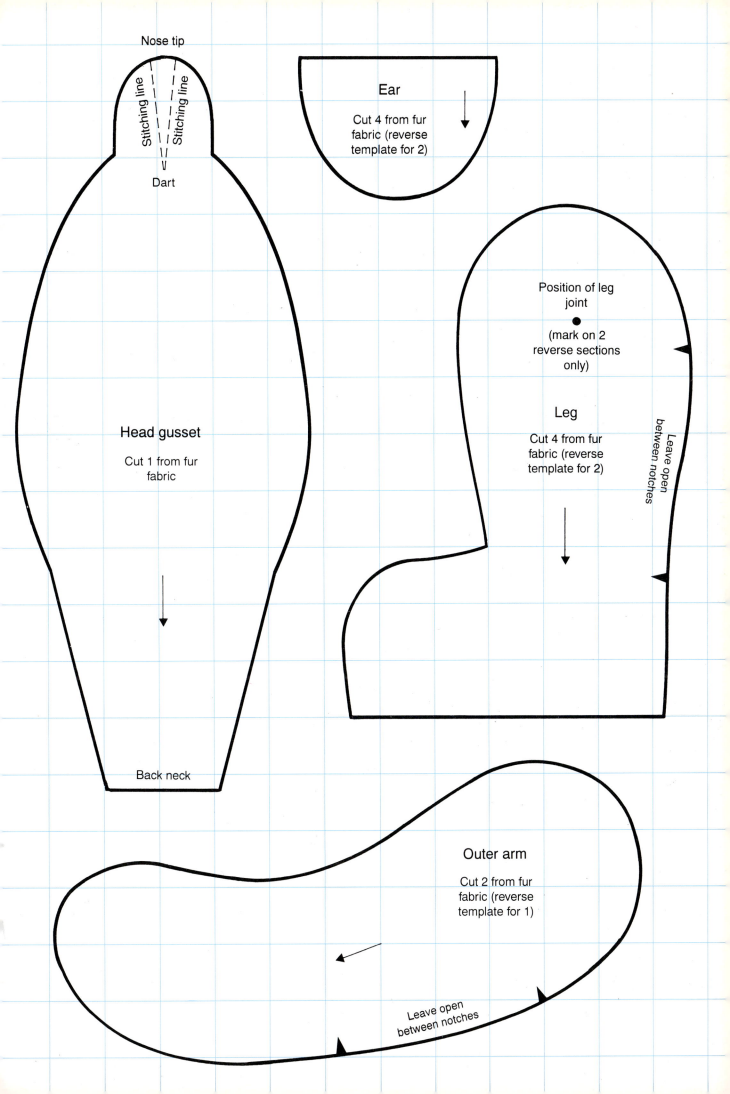

Bear Care

A bear should be a lifelong companion. Appropriate cleaning and storage will ensure that your bears stay in top condition.

Cleaning Most bears need only occasional, gentle cleaning with a vacuum cleaner on a low-power setting to remove loose dust. Use a nozzle attachment that has been screened by a piece of nylon gauze stretched over the end and firmly secured with a rubber band. This will prevent any loose eyes or ears from being sucked into the dust bag.

Bears that have become more severely soiled can be sponged with mild soap suds. Unless your bear has been made entirely with washable materials (see *Samuel*, page 100), it is essential that the filling, whether woodwool, sawdust or kapok, should not become damp. Once sponged clean, put your bear into an airing cupboard (or a similar warm, dry place) on lots of clean, dry towels to dry slowly. Do not tumble dry or place near a direct source of heat such as a radiator or convector fire.

Some specialist bear-supply suppliers stock aerosol cans of bear-conditioning and cleaning solutions. These are sprayed on and lightly sponged away. Follow the manufacturers' instructions when using such products.

Insect infestation Some old bears may become a host to small insects and mites. The safest treatment for this problem is to place the bear in a well-sealed plastic bag and leave it in the freezer for a few days. If the bear has glass eyes, however, it might be best to remove these first as old glass

> A useful tip when making bears is to put a pair of extra ear shapes into the body of the bear whilst stuffing. In later years, if an ear becomes detached, a replacement can be found with no difficulty, provided of course that the owner knows about the hiding place.

can be fragile and should be preserved at all costs. Replace the eyes when the bear has regained room temperature.

Storage Bears stored away from the light should be wrapped in acid-free tissue paper. A few moth balls can be popped into the drawer or box as an added precaution (see also the box on page 12). Do not use cardboard, brown paper or newspaper to store bears made from natural fabrics, as the acid emitted by these materials can eventually rot the material.

Repairs When it comes to repair work, the motto must be 'little is best'. For drastic repairs such as split paws and pads, an oval of fabric stitched over the original is the best choice wherever possible. If the damage is extensive, however, always keep any fabric that has been removed, so that it can be replaced again if necessary.

Tears in the fur pile should be covered with a small patch of fabric, which can be oversewn into position. Split seams and even gaps around pads and paws can usually be successfully ladder-stitched together.

In the case of a lost eye, you need to decide whether to replace one or both eyes. If you choose to replace the pair, always keep the original eye somewhere safe. The other may always turn up, or a close match may be found later.

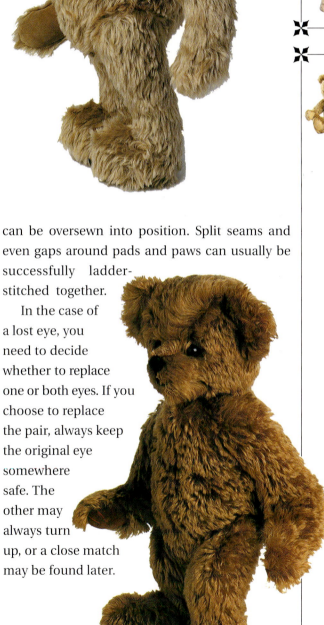

Useful Addresses

Suppliers of bear-making materials

UNITED KINGDOM

Christie Bears
92 The Green
Kings Norton
Birmingham B38 8 RS
Tel: 0121-459 8817

Comprehensive range of mohair, felt and other bear-making items.

Nonsuch Soft Toys
The Gables
King Edward Road
Axminster
Devon EX13 5PP
Tel: 01297-35017

Suppliers of a comprehensive range of superb Yorkshire and German mohairs. Some exclusive colours.

Patricia Woods
Mulberry Silks
2 Old Rectory Cottage
Easton Grey
Malmesbury
Wiltshire SN16 0PE
Tel: 0666-840 881

Supplier of high quality pure silk embroidery threads in a full range of colours and shades.

S. Glassner
476 Kingston Road
Raynes Park
London SW20 8DX
Tel: 0181-543 1666

Leather, tooling and modelling implements and heavy linen threads.

J & J Cash Ltd.
Torrington Avenue
Coventry CV4 9UZ
Tel: 0203-466 466

Woven fabric name-tapes, care labels and designer labels.

USA

Bear Clawset
27 Palermo Walk
Long Beach
California 90803

Carver's Eye Co.
PO Box 16692
Portland
Oregon 97216
Tel: (503) 666 5680

Wide selection of eyes suitable for bears, dolls, etc. Suppliers of recessed plastic eyes that create an eye socket.

Edinburgh Imports, Inc.
PO Box 722, Department F
Woodland Hills
California 91365-0722
Tel: (818) 591 3806

Suppliers of over 500 fabrics, including tipped, wavy and feathered.

Bucilla
1 Oak Ridge Road
Hazelton
Pennsylvania 18201-9764
Tel: (717) 384 2525

Suppliers of silk ribbons for embroidering claws and noses.

THE NETHERLANDS

Berenatelier Ferrageau de Saint Amand
Wielemakersslop 6
Voorburg

Atelier "Nikkie Bear"
Dorpsweg 66a
Rotterdam 3083 LD
Tel: 010-481 6022

Mohair fabrics, ribbons and accessories for miniature bears.

GERMANY

Anna Teddy
26160 Bad Zwischenahn
Peterstrasse 2
Tel: 04403-65936

Fabrics, eyes, antique bears and newsletter.

Barenhaus
Sabine Strohbach & Christel Hinterding
Gruner Weg 83
48268 Greven
Tel: 02571-40243

A wide range of high-quality mohairs and unusual cotton fabrics. Also suppliers of accessories, clothing and other bear items.

Organizations

The British Toymakers' Guild
124 Walcot Street
Bath
Avon BA1 5BG
ENGLAND
Tel: 01225-442440

British Standards Institution
Linford Wood
Milton Keynes
MK14 6LE.

British Teddy Bear Association
PO Box 290
Brighton BN2 1DR

Good Bears of the World (UK)
53 Marble Hill Close
Twickenham
Middlesex TW1 3AY
ENGLAND
Tel: 0181-891 5746.

and

Good Bears of the World
PO Box 13097
Toledo
Ohio 43613
USA

Registered charity sending teddy bears worldwide to help sick children and those in need of special comfort.

Club Francais de l'Ours Ancien
Aline Cousin
Boite 7082
70 Rue du Docteur
Sureau 93160
Noisy Le Grand
FRANCE.

Bear-buying

Julia Jones Classic Bears
PO Box 16
Swadlincote
Derbyshire DE 12 8ZZ
ENGLAND.

For specially commissioned bears, after dinner speaking engagements, lectures, "Classic Bear" workshops and craft-based holidays in Derbyshire and Sussex.

Christie's Auction Rooms
5 Old Brompton Road
London SW7 3LD
ENGLAND

For advice on all aspects of buying and selling collectors' bears at auction. Annual Teddy Bear Auction (usually held in early December). Auctions of dolls, toys and other memorabilia take place regularly at Christie's in South Kensington. A calendar of sale dates is available on request.

Museums and displays

Margarete Steiff Museum
Giegen (Brenz)
Nr Stuttgart
GERMANY

Permanent display of old teddy bears and dolls.

Bethnal Green Museum of Childhood
Cambridge Heath Road
London E2 9PA
ENGLAND
Tel: 0181-981 1711

Bournemouth Bears
Old Christchurch Lane
Bournemouth BH1 1NE
ENGLAND
Tel: 01202 293 544

Pollock's Toy Museum
1 Scala Street
London W1P 1LT
ENGLAND
Tel: 0171-636 3452

The Teddy Bear Museum
19 Greenhill Street
Stratford-on-Avon CV37 6LF
ENGLAND
Tel: 01789-293 160

The Margaret Woodbury Strong Museum
One Manhattan Square
Rochester
New York 14607
USA

Romy's Bazaar
2 Badgery's Crescent
Lawson 2783
AUSTRALIA

Further Reading

Bearland, Deborah Stratton (Michael O'Mara Books Ltd, 1993)

Button in the Ear, J. & M. Cieslik (Cieslik Publishing, 1989)

Collector's Guide to Teddy Bears, Peter Ford (Quarto Publishing, 1994)

Pollock's History of English Dolls & Toys, Kenneth and Marguerite Fawdry (Ernest Benn, 1979)

Teddy Bear, Gustav Severin (Ellert & Richter Verlag, Hamburg, 1992, and Transedition Books, 1994)

The Bear Lover's Guide to Britain, Pat Rush (Pan Books, 1994)

The Ultimate Teddy Bear Book, Pauline Cockrill (Dorling Kindersley, 1991)

UK Teddy Bear Guide 1995 (Hugglets)

PERIODICALS
Teddy Bear Scene
7 Ferringham Lane
Ferring
West Sussex BN 12 5ND
ENGLAND
Tel: 01903-506626

Magazine published six times a year.

National Doll & Teddy Bear Collector
PO Box 4032
Portland
Oregon 97208-4032
USA

Full-colour monthly newspaper featuring teddy bears.

Teddy Bear and Friends
PO Box 467
Mount Morris
Illinois 61054-7896
USA

Bear Facts Review
PO Box 503
Moss Vale
NSW 2577
AUSTRALIA

Bi-annual teddy bear magazine.

In Teddies We Trust
PO Box 297
Rosebery
Sydney, 2018 NSW
AUSTRALIA

Beer Bericht Magazine
Prinsengracht 1089
1017 JH Amsterdam
THE NETHERLANDS

Teddy bear magazine, with free translation for overseas subscribers.

BOOKSHOP
"Images"
The Staffs Bookshop
4 & 6 Dam Street
Lichfield
Staffordshire WS13 6AA
ENGLAND
Tel: 01543-264093

Books on the history and making of teddy bears and associated crafts, including those published in the USA, the UK, Germany and France. Mailing service. Catalogue available on request.

INDEX

Algie 20–33
alpaca 9
angora 10
arms 14, 28
assembling pattern pieces 23–5
Astbury 52–7

basic bear 20–33
Bertie 64–71
brushes 19, 31

cashmere 9, 11
Charles 40–5
Claude 46–51
claws 31
clothed bears 74
cutting board 17
cutting out 23

dark bears 80

ears 29
Edward 86–93
embroidery 12, 14, 19, 30, 31
equipment 16–19
expressions 43, 54
eyes 15, 28–9, 34

fabric 8, 9–12, 66
    amount required 22
    cutting 23, 42
    recycling 72, 78
felt 11–12, 86
female bears 8, 42, 72–7
fillings 12–13
fleece 12
forceps 19
fraying 11

German bears 48
glasses 15, 16

growlers 15, 94–7

interfacing 11, 12

joints 14, 22, 26–7, 100

kapok 12

labels 18
leather 11, 18
legs 14, 28
lining fabric 11, 42
Little Roger 58–63

markers 17
materials 8–19
miniature bears 8, 34, 36
mohair 10
    distressed-pile 40, 46
    long-pile 52, 100
moths 12
mouth 30
musical boxes 15, 86–93
muzzle 25, 26, 29–30

needles 18
noses 15, 30, 46, 54, 67–8

Oscar 94–9

pads/paws 11, 23, 27
paper/card 17
patterns
    adapting 46, 58
    enlarging 21
    transferring 22–3
pens 17
pile 8, 10, 22, 24, 42
pin cushion 18
pins 18
plastic pellets 12, 66
pliers 18–19

Roger, Little 58-63
Rose 72–7
rulers 17

safety 9, 14, 15, 16, 18, 102
Samuel 100–5
sawdust 13, 40
scissors 16–17
seam allowances 24
seam ripper 19
sewing machine 16
silk 10, 11, 72
squeakers 16, 94
stands 19
stitches 19
stuffing 12, 26–8
stuffing tools 17
suede/suedette 11
synthetic fabrics 8, 10–11, 66, 102

tape-measure 17
templates 21–2
Theodore 78–85
thimble 18
thread 13–14
Tiny 34–9
tracing wheel 17–18
tweezers 19

velvet 12, 64, 81
voices 15, 86, 94–7

white bears 60
woodwool 13

111

Acknowledgements

The author would like to thank the following for their unceasing help and encouragement, as well as practical assistance and advice, in the preparation of this book: David and Sue Rixon of Nonsuch Bears, and Anne Stevens of Christie Bears for providing me with some of the materials used for making my bears. Patricia Woods at Mulberry Silks for her help and advice in choosing silks suitable for noses and claws. And Carol Hammond for pattern reading and for making up Oscar. Rose Wharnsby at Good Bears of the World for her kindness. Also my mother, Roger and Pam Smith, John Evans, Dawn, Terry and Emma Kirtland, and my children Matthew and Esther once again for all their support. In addition, the author would like to thank all at Dragon's World for their hard work and enthusiasm. And finally a special thanks to Esther Jones for her patience and skill in taking the photographs used to produce the step-by-step drawings.

The publisher would like to thank the following suppliers who provided materials and props for the photographs:

Lunn Antiques Ltd
86 New Kings Road
London SW6 4LU

Tel: 0171-736 4638

Finch & Fryer Lighting
88 Wandsworth Bridge Road
London SW6 2TF

Tel: 0171-731 8886

Henry Gregory
82 Portobello Road
London W11 2QD

Tel: 0171-792 9221

Paperchase
213 Tottenham Court Road
London W1P 9AF

Tel: 0171-580 8496

The London Dolls House Company
29 Covent Garden Market
London WC2 8RE

Tel: 0171-240 8681